A WORKING DOG'S TALE!

by *Vince Raw*

VINCE RAW

As told by a springer spaniel called

Bess

GALLOWAY COTTAGES PUBLISHING

This book is copyright. Enquiries should be addressed to Vince Raw,
c/o Galloway Cottages Publishing, Stronord, Newton Stewart,
DG8 7BD, Scotland
e-mail gallowaycottages@aol.com

Copyright ©Vince Raw 2004

The right of Vince Raw to be identified as the author of this work has
been asserted in accordance with the Copyright, Design and Patents
Act 1988

ISBN 0-9539086-3-1

All rights reserved. This book is sold subject to the condition that it
shall not be reproduced, stored in a retrieval system or transmitted, in
any form or by any means, electronic, photocopying, recording or
otherwise without the prior written permission of the author. Nor shall
it by way of trade or otherwise be lent, resold, hired out or otherwise
circulated without the author's prior consent in any form of binding or
cover other than that in which it is published.

A catalogue record for this book is available from the British Library

Published by Galloway Cottages Publishing

Front cover illustration by Victoria Hornby
Back cover illustration by Angie Joint

Printed and bound by J. W. Arrowsmith Ltd., Bristol, England

CONTENTS

	Preface	5
1.	Opening my eyes	7
2.	Meeting Grob	14
3.	Trials and Trivialization	22
4.	First day beating	27
5.	The Ouse Washes	42
6.	Beating and the Christmas party	57
7.	The Boxing Day shoot	74
8.	Geese on Wigtown Bay	88
9.	Keeper's day with Laurel and Hardy	102

ACKNOWLEDGEMENTS

Vince Raw would like to sincerely thank the following for their help and co-operation relating to this book.

Jennie Raw, for her patience, help and constant encouragement.

Tony and Pat Wallace, for their continuing friendship and their tremendous contributions to this book.

Victoria Hornby and Angie Joint, for their kindness in providing the artwork for the cover.

J W Arrowsmith Ltd, for their help with the printing of this book.

**Other titles by the author,
published by Galloway Cottages Publishing**

"It'll be alright on the flight!"
"On the flight again!"

PREFACE

If you are anything like me your dog, or dogs in my case, will be very special creatures indeed. But how many of us take the time to consider how a dog thinks? We just give the orders and expect the dog to obey without question. It is true that most of the time they do what we ask, but not without question. What we don't seem to realise is that the dogs communicate with each other, just like us humans. Well, they do in this book and it gives a great insight into how they see us for what we do and for what we are.

This story is told by a springer spaniel called Bess. It starts from the beginning and delves well into her life. She was a working dog and proud of it, accompanying me on many shooting adventures. Whether it was wildfowling, pigeon or rough shooting, driven pheasants or partridge, picking up or just humble beating, she still showed the same enthusiasm.

What we do not realise is that the dogs have a great sense of humour and the way they communicate with each other is hilarious. She meets lots of different breeds of dogs in the course of her work and some of them are incredible characters. Amongst the many is a Jack Russell who loves to fight, and an Irish water spaniel who loves to swear.

It is interesting to hear what the dogs think about us and each other, and Bess tells her story with humour foremost in her mind.

As well as keeping some of the human characters from my other books in the stories there are also a number of new ones included and they all add to the humour.

The dogs feel emotion and can fall in love like us. You may see your dog differently after reading this.

Vince Raw

The original Bess

A WORKING DOG'S TALE!

CHAPTER 1

Opening my eyes

The first time I opened my eyes I was in a shed with three sisters and two brothers. It all seemed a bit overcrowded to me, especially at meal times. There never seemed to be enough teats to go round and I often found that after forcing my way through for one I would find it was empty. One of my brothers was nearly twice the size of me and going by his mannerisms he should really have been born into a litter of pigs. We called him Podgy because of his size. He was extremely aggressive and greedy and was nothing but a nuisance to us all, including our mum.

Mum wouldn't let anyone near us at first and I felt really secure knowing that she would protect me. However, as time went on she became more impatient with us and seemed to take every opportunity to leave us on our own. Podgy took full advantage of these situations and expressed his authority on us by biting our ears and making us yelp.

The more our natural mum left us the more time our new mum would spend with us. She was lovely, giving us food and cuddles. She was different to us though, having just two legs. And instead of having a hairy coat with patches on like us she had red hair on her head, no hair on her face and hands and wore clothes covering the rest of her body.

As the weeks passed by we all started growing and were rapidly catching up with Podgy. One day Podgy decided to bite me viciously and I started yelping. My other brother came from behind him and took a mouthful of his ear, dragging him backwards across the shed floor. Well, the noise that came out of Podgy's mouth was incredible. Our new mum came running in and grabbed hold of my other brother which made him let go of Podgy, who was still yelping. She told my brother off and gave him a shake. That was the first injustice to a dog that I witnessed, but there would be many more to come in my lifetime.

One day when we were seven weeks old our new mum seemed to be very excited as she cleaned out our shed and the run. We had new bedding and our dishes were washed. We were then picked up and brushed. A little while later she returned with a man who spent a lot of time looking at us. After picking us all up individually and looking into our ears and eyes he stood there as though he was pondering. Mum then took a little ball out of her pocket and rolled it along the floor. I would have run after it but I saw Podgy setting off and there was no way I was going to upset him, so like the others, I stayed where I was. Podgy was quick at getting to the ball and without any further hesitation the man pointed at Podgy and said, 'I will take that one. He is a bold strong dog and I like the black and white markings.' The man picked Podgy up and as they walked away Podgy peed down the man's trousers. I never saw Podgy again for a number of years but life was considerably better without him. The next day when our natural mum paid us a brief visit she explained that we will all go like Podgy did, but we shouldn't worry about it because it would be much better than living in the shed.

During the course of the next two weeks we had many visits from people. The routine was very much the same. The visitor would pick us up for an examination and mum would roll the ball. The person who was looking at us nearly always selected the one that got to the ball first and now there were just three of us left. When there were six of us we snuggled up to each other but now it was different and quite cold during the night. Our natural mum had disowned us by now and although she often walked past the run she virtually ignored us, despite our rapid tail wagging.

The next week we had several visits from people and although I got to the ball first I was not selected. Each time there would be similar comments about my markings. I was liver and white but instead of having liver markings evenly situated around my eyes and ears I had a white patch at the side of one of my eyes that spread on to half of my ear.

The sad day came when I was on my own in the shed and I lay there feeling very miserable. My natural mum occasionally came to look at me, and although I asked her to stay she walked away each time. I was lonely and frightened during the night, with just a brown rat for company.

I was nearly eight weeks old when a man came to look. He picked me up and stroked me gently. I licked him and he cuddled me. When he put me down I sat on his foot. Mum took the ball out of her pocket and rolled it. I knew the routine by now and ran after it. After I had carried it back the man picked me up again and spent some time looking at my face and the white marking. Here we go again, I thought, but to my delight he said, 'I am not bothered about the markings, I will take her.'

I was carried into my mum's house and the man sat down on a chair with me on his lap. My natural mum was in there lying on a blanket in a basket. She came across and I thought she had come to see me but all she wanted was the man to stroke her. My mum gave the man some papers and as he got up to leave she said, 'What are you going to call her Vince?' My new master replied, 'She is going to be called Bess and she will be a working dog as well as a pet.' I now knew my name and that of my new dad. I was so excited that I lost control of my bladder and did the same thing that Podgy had done on my new dad's trousers.

When we reached the car dad put me in a little cardboard box, which had a blanket in the bottom, and it was placed on the front passenger seat. Dad dried his trousers but he wasn't angry with me. Even when I was sick in the box he still wasn't angry. We seemed to be in the car for a long time and went round a lot of corners and up and down some steep hills. I would have been sick some more but there was nothing left inside me to bring up, it was all on the blanket in the box and I was sitting in it.

We eventually stopped outside a three-storey house. Dad picked me up and took me inside the house and up a flight of stairs to the middle floor. It was then that I met Jennie, my new mum. Dad passed me to her and she kissed me. She quickly handed me back and remarked that I stank of sick. I was then given a wash followed by something to eat with some milk to drink. I kept eating a bit and then drinking a bit but I couldn't stop looking round at my new mum and dad who were watching me in a loving way.

When I had eaten as much as I could I was taken back down the stairs and out the back door into a garden. There was a lawn surrounded with flower beds and a shed situated at the bottom. The garden was full of interesting smells and I spent time wandering around checking them all out. I then did a pooh on the grass and dad was delighted with me, telling me what a good girl I was. I couldn't understand what all the fuss was about. After all, I had been doing poohs several times a day since I had been born. Dad took me back inside and told mum what I had done. She kissed me and told me I was a very good girl.

I followed them into the living room which was ten times the size of the shed I had lived in. It had a thick pile carpet and a cosy rug in front of a fire. After all the excitement I was feeling rather tired and decided to curl up on the rug and go to sleep for a while.

When I woke up some time later mum and dad were watching the television and were not looking at me. I thought I would please them and attract their attention so I had a wee on the carpet. I couldn't believe what happened next. Mum shouted 'Oh no! She is weeing on the carpet.' Dad leapt out of his chair and grabbed hold of me. He was running down the stairs with me in his arms and all the time telling me I was a very naughty girl. We went out the back door and I was dumped unceremoniously onto the grass and told to do it there. I was so frightened I had to have a pooh and suddenly dad was telling me I was a good girl again. He picked me up and carried me back up the stairs into the living room. I licked his face on the way and that seemed to please him. He told mum that I had done another pooh on the grass and she kissed me again.

I lay back on the rug to try and work this out. After all, I did want to be a good girl and get the praise. When I did the wee I was a naughty girl and was told off but when I did the pooh I was a good girl and was kissed. That's the answer, I thought, the next time I want a pooh I will do it on the carpet where they both can see me. I should be a really good girl then. All this weeing and poohing and thinking tactics was making me tired again so I decided to go back to sleep on the rug. As I was dozing I lifted my eyelids and mum and dad were both watching me and smiling. This is much better than that lonely shed, I thought, and wagged my tail as I drifted off to sleep.

When I woke up they were still there. I must have slept for a long time because I could see through the windows that it was now dark outside. I had a bit of a problem though because I needed a wee and they were watching me. I didn't want to get into trouble so I thought I would sneak behind the armchair and do one. I set off for my chosen spot but dad spotted me and picked me up before I got there. He then took me into the garden again. He put me on the grass and stood watching me. I couldn't hold it any longer and had to do it. He picked me up again and cuddled me telling me how good I was and then back upstairs for more kisses from mum. I was now very confused because

I thought I got told off when I had a wee. I knew I was a good girl when I did a pooh and couldn't wait to please them again.

Well, my chance came two hours later. I managed to squeeze one out in the middle of the rug and stood back waiting for the praise. Dad went potty. He grabbed me and pointed to the little heap telling me how naughty I was. I was then taken to the garden and showed the grass again. I was totally confused with the whole situation and decided that it would be better if I didn't wee or pooh ever again.

Night time came and I was put in a basket in the kitchen. It was warm and cosy but mum and dad went upstairs and left me on my own. I had been through a very funny day. I had been rescued from the shed where I was born. I had inherited a new mum and dad, who didn't seem to be sure whether I was a good girl or a naughty girl. I am now on my own in the kitchen where they have put newspaper on the floor. I wasn't sure whether I was expected to read it or wee on it, so I decided to howl.

After a while dad came down and stroked me and told me to be quiet. When he had gone back I waited ten minutes and then howled again, but twice as loud. This time mum came down. She cuddled me and put a teddy bear in my basket next to me. It didn't seem to mind when I chewed its ears and after a while I cuddled up to it and went to sleep. Mum must have crept out because I never heard her go.

I woke up as it was breaking light. I could hear mum and dad walking about upstairs and I started to get excited. Unfortunately, this had an adverse effect on my bladder and even though I had decided I was never going to do it again I wandered around the room looking for a suitable place and eventually squatted down on the newspaper where I produced a little pool. Climbing back in my basket I waited for them to come down, expecting another telling off. When mum came in she seemed pleased. She told me I was a good girl for having a wee on the paper, but before I could please her even more by doing a pooh for her dad arrived and took me into the garden. I did one on the lawn and I was a good girl again. It was all too much for me to understand so I forgot all about it and waited for my breakfast.

After breakfast dad went off to work. During the day mum took me into the garden every half-hour. I spent a lot of time hunting where mice had been and attacking the odd spider and butterfly. I also managed a few wees and poohs and that made mum happy. When dad came home he made a fuss of me and I slept on his lap until bedtime. I was settling in nicely. I had even managed to chase a cat out of the garden. Life was good in my new home.

Over the next few weeks I got the idea of doing my wees and poohs in the garden. And apart from the very odd mistake I was mainly house clean. Dad spent a lot of time with me in the garden throwing dummies for me to fetch. Sometimes he would let me fetch them and other times he made me sit while he retrieved them himself. This was the start of my basic training to be my dad's companion in the sport that he loved, which was shooting.

When I was twelve weeks old dad took me to see a vet. He seemed a nice sort of man so I wagged my tail and licked him. He repaid my affection by sticking a big needle in me. When we went back a fortnight later I didn't wag my tail. In fact, when I saw him I tried to make a run for it. Dad held me and the vet stuck another needle in me. I will never trust a man in a white coat again.

Once that was over and done with dad took me out a lot and I enjoyed all the different smells of the countryside. I also encountered a few bullies like Podgy but dad was quick to chase them away. Over the next few months I was taught how to sit when dad blew his whistle a certain way and how to hunt and come in on the whistle. The good thing was we both enjoyed it. It was good for me because I had all the hunting to do while dad just stood there. He seemed to be happy with the situation so it was all right by me.

When I was ten months old dad took me out with his gun. I had seen dad with the gun before but he had always left me at home. He would often bring a dead rabbit back and throw it for me to retrieve. He would also hide the rabbit from me and I would have to find it. He was always pleased with me when I found it so I liked that game.

This time when we went out dad stopped and collected his friend Tony on the way and we walked across some fields. I wanted to hunt but dad made me stay in to heel. After a while dad said to Tony, 'We had better make sure she is not gun shy.' He told me to sit and Tony took the gun about fifty yards away. He fired it and it went off with a bang. Dad looked at me and I looked at him. Dad seemed to be pleased and asked Tony to come in closer. He then fired the gun again. Dad looked at me again and I couldn't understand what was going on. Dad had a chat with Tony and they both seemed to be pleased with me.

We walked over a field of stubble and although it was ideal hunting country dad made me stay to heel. After a while some birds took to the air and Tony put the gun up and fired. To my surprise no sooner had the gun gone off with a bang when a bird fell out of the sky and on to the field of stubble. I looked up at dad and he was watching me. After a while he told me to fetch. I ran off to where the bird had dropped and soon saw it. Picking it up I ran back to dad. He took it off me and made a big fuss of me. The bird was a partridge and that was my first warm retrieve. I was ready for more but dad said that would do for now and we all went back home. I lay in front of the fire that night while listening to dad telling mum all about my retrieve. I must admit I couldn't help wagging my tail.

I learnt that certain things I did pleased them, while other things didn't. I got into the habit of picking up my food bowl when I had finished eating. They thought this was really clever and gave me a stroke. What they didn't realise is it was my way of asking for more.

One day they were both looking miserable. Dad was in a bad mood so I thought I would try and cheer them up. My food bowl wasn't there but my water bowl was. It was in its usual place, on the landing at the top of the stairs. I picked it up and took it into the sitting room to show them. Unfortunately, all the water spilt out and dad did his pieces. Dad told mum to get a heavier bowl as he stormed off to work without stroking me.

Mum went shopping and came back with a big heavy bowl. She put some water in it and put it on the landing. I remember thinking, I could have a swim in that. The next morning when dad was going to work he tripped over the bowl, which went tumbling down the stairs spilling the water as it went. Dad banged his head on the wall and his face turned every shade of red. I sensed that there could be trouble and dived under the table in the kitchen and crossed my legs to control my bladder. Dad carried on down the stairs and shouted, 'When I said get a bigger bowl I didn't mean a bloody dustbin lid!' He slammed the door on his way out and mum sat in the chair and started laughing. I jumped on her lap and chuckled myself. I knew dad hated going to work because he was a much nicer person at the weekends when we were going out together.

CHAPTER 2

Meeting Grob

It was a Friday night and I was sitting on dad's lap. He was telling me that we were going to go out the next day with Tony, and that they were going to try and shoot some pigeons. He also told me that Tony had a dog like me. I was looking forward to going as I lay in my basket that night. I liked being with mum and dad but I hadn't spent any time with another dog for months. I was wondering if Tony's dog might be one of my sisters.

The next morning dad was up early and was in a very good mood. He was singing as he was taking his gun out of the cabinet. He brought a sack full of something out of the shed and that was thrown in the back of the car. Mum made a packed lunch and I was pleased to see some of my favourite biscuits going in. I was becoming really excited and decided to stay very close to dad, just in case he forgot to take me. Unfortunately, he turned quickly and not knowing I was right behind him he tripped over me and dropped the packed lunch on the kitchen floor. He shouted at me and I ran under the table. Mum then threw the broken thermos flask away and found another one.

Five minutes later we were on our way to Tony's house and dad was in a good mood again. When we arrived we went in and Tony was sitting at the table in the kitchen rolling a cigarette. His wife Pat was cooking something that smelt very good. She made a fuss of me and made them some tea. I was sitting on the floor wondering where the other dog was. I could smell dogs but there wasn't one there.

After a while Tony stood up and said, 'I will go and fetch Grobally.' He went outside and while he was gone Pat stroked me. I was just thinking how nice it was there when Tony opened the door. A spaniel's head that was far bigger than I had ever seen before peered round the door. He had a rugged looking face and hungry looking eyes that stared straight at me. He then said, 'Bugger me, young crumpet.' and made a beeline for me. I ran under the table to get behind dad's legs. That didn't deter him and he chased after me drooling from the mouth. I was frightened and started crying. Tony grabbed him and pulled him out from under the table and I stayed put behind my dad's legs. Tony dragged him to the other side of the kitchen and shouted at him, telling him to stay. This didn't seem to bother Grobally at all and I knew he was just waiting for the chance to get at me by the look on his face.

Tony eventually put his coat on and took his gun out of a cupboard. Grobally seemed to get excited and lost interest in me, or so I thought. As we were walking down the path to the car he pounced. He said, 'Let's see what you have got my lovely.' He then stuck his nose under my belly and turned me over onto my back in a second. I just lay there petrified while he checked out all my private bits. He then said, 'You're a nice little thing. You can call me Grob if you want.' I said 'All right Grob, my name is Bess but please don't hurt me.' He said, 'I won't hurt you pretty one. I am going to look after you!'

When we were in the car Tony was telling dad that there was a lot of wild game on the farm where we were going, but today they were just shooting pigeons. After leaving the car in the farmyard we walked down a track and across some fields. Grob started quartering so I joined in. I noticed that the smell on the ground was the same smell as that of the partridge that I had picked up last time I was out and seconds later a covey took to the air in front of us. I looked over to Grob and saw him sit. I thought I had better do the same thing and dad shouted good girl as I did. I decided that I would watch Grob as he would probably teach me a thing or two.

The next field we walked across I found myself in trouble. Grob and I were quartering and I was really enjoying it. There was lots of scent and I was waiting for the next covey of partridges to get up when suddenly a hare leapt up just five yards in front of us. This was the first one I had ever seen. I looked across at Grob and he looked as though he was about to go after it. I fixed my eyes on the hare and set off like a whippet. What I hadn't noticed was that Grob had had second thoughts and decided against the chase. I was twenty yards out and going like a train when dad screamed at me. I stopped in my tracks and sat. Dad came over and I could see he was angry. I was in deep trouble and there was no table here to hide under. He took a handful of loose skin at each side of my neck and dragged me back to where Grob was sitting. Looking straight into my eyes he shouted 'NO' to me five times. When he let go of me I looked across at Grob and he was laughing at me. So much for him looking after me!

We walked across two more fields to get to where they were going to shoot the pigeons and while Grob was hunting away enjoying himself I had to walk to heel. I was beginning to wish I had never seen the damned hare.

The field had rape just peeping through the ground and several hundred pigeons took to the air as we approached. Tony and dad built a hide in the hedge and then dad emptied the bag he had been carrying. I was surprised to see that they were plastic birds and watched them being positioned about thirty yards away from the hide. While this was all going on Grob was trying his best to have his wicked way with me. Every time Tony turned around to look at him he was sitting there with an innocent look on his face, but every time Tony turned away again the randy sod was trying to seduce me.

We all went into the hide and they took their guns out of the slips. Grob took up the position of lookout to the rear and was sitting there staring intently through the hedge. I found a little hole in the front of the hide so I could see up the field.

We didn't have to wait long before twenty pigeons flew over where the plastic ones were. Both guns went off and two pigeons fell to the ground. That's good, I thought, I had better go and get them. Dad must have been watching me because as I went to move I was sternly told to stay.

Minutes later more pigeons were out in front. Dad shot one as they were coming towards us and as they climbed up after dad's shot Tony shot one that dropped just three yards in front of me. I really wanted to go for it and looked up at dad. He was watching me and then said 'Fetch'. I ran out of the hide and picked the pigeon up. It was absolutely horrible. I had a mouthful of loose feathers which seemed to stick to my mouth and one was in my throat. I dropped the pigeon on the ground and started to try and spit the feathers out of my mouth. I heard the stern voice of dad saying, 'Fetch.' I decided I had better do what I was told so I picked it up and took it in the hide where I spat it out at dad's feet. This made Grob roar with laughter. Dad was not happy with me and stepped back two paces. He said, 'Now fetch' and held his hand out. I picked it up again and took it to him. He took it from me and gave me a big hug. 'What a good girl you are,' he said, and looked very pleased. I soon got rid of the feathers and realised that they weren't that bad and that I had actually enjoyed it in the end.

Unfortunately, I spent most of the day in the hide watching. When they had shot a dozen pigeons they brought in the plastic ones and went out and pegged up the dead birds with sticks cut from the hedge. During this short period I nearly lost my virginity with Grob taking full advantage of the cover from the hide.

The shooting went on for about three hours before the pigeons decided that they would feed somewhere else. Tony was shooting well but dad kept complaining that he didn't know how he was missing them. Grob said to me, 'Take no notice of your dad Bess. He always misses them and says that.' We both burst out laughing. It's a good job they can't hear us talking to each other or we would be in trouble.

When the pigeons were coming in from behind Grob would tell me. He would then wag his tail to let the men know. Good shooting was had at some of those birds offering different angles. When it was all over Grob and I were allowed to go out and bring the dead birds in. That took us about five minutes and I really enjoyed it, getting some praise every time I brought one to hand. It's strange how I forgot about the loose feathers so quickly.

Back at Tony's house we were all in the kitchen. Grob and I were lying on the floor listening to Tony and dad talking about the day and I started to feel quite drowsy. Grob was across the other side of the kitchen and looking at me. He grinned at me as we both lay there listening to the chat. He said, 'They could go on for hours once they start reminiscing. I am going to sleep.'

They started talking about dogs that they had had in the past and Dad told Tony and Pat a story about ferreting with two Jack Russell terriers called Digger and Bruce that he used to have.

It was when he was much younger and he had a friend called Kenny who was keen on ferreting. Kenny had told him that he had managed to obtain permission to go ferreting on some ground just outside Luton. With the ferrets in a box, a good sharp little spade for digging and a couple of dozen purse nets in their pockets they were ready to go.

The form of transport was a pick-up truck, which belonged to the builder who they were both working for at that time. This truck had a small rear window in the cab, that is, it was supposed to have a small rear window but the glass had been knocked out some years before by a sliding load and it had never been replaced. After scraping the ice from the screen they eventually got started. It was freezing with the cold air circulating around their ears from the missing window behind their heads.

As dad drove the truck Kenny had Digger and Bruce sitting on his knee and both dogs were trembling with excitement. As soon as they had seen the ferret box they knew what was going to happen. They didn't particularly like ferrets but they didn't mind working with a good one. Dad had found this out to his embarrassment a few weeks previously when a young man called Alan went out with him with the intentions of trying out his new ferret. Digger and Bruce were marking the holes where the rabbits were while dad and Alan were setting the nets. As Alan put the ferret in a hole the dogs were shaking and ready to pounce.

The ferret was useless and it just kept coming out and wandering about on top. After this had happened on about ten different occasions it was too much for the Jack Russells to take. As the ferret wandered past Digger he grabbed hold of it, gave it a shake and threw it up in the air as if he was trying to tell it to do its job properly. The squeals from the ferret seemed to excite Bruce and he joined in with the fun. Every time the ferret landed one of them grabbed it and threw it up in the air again. Alan looked horrified but was frightened to interfere in case the ferocious little miniatures set about him. Dad was becoming very concerned now because the dogs were definitely getting rougher and were beginning to fight with each other to decide which one had the privilege of throwing the ferret next.

He dived on top of the ferret to protect it. The smell that came from it was indescribable and it soaked into his clothes in seconds. To make things worse the ferret bit him as he got hold of it, which caused him to yell and shake it off. As the ferret hit the ground Digger was on it again like lightning. Once again dad had to rescue the ungrateful ferret, thinking to himself that it was a pity it wasn't so aggressive with rabbits as it was with him.

The ferret survived the ordeal but dad doubted if it would ever trust a dog again. When he arrived home he had to strip off all of his clothes and put them in the washing machine. He then soaked his body in a bath full of hot soapy water to try and get rid of the dreadful smell. When he climbed out of the bath the dogs went in next.

They arrived at their destination in the pickup truck and Kenny directed dad to park on the grass verge at the side of the road. After walking across a couple of fields they were soon checking out small warrens but the dogs showed no interest at the holes. Eventually, they did find some holes where Digger showed an interest. They set the nets and dad placed one of the ferrets on the edge of the hole. It gave itself a shake, then had a sniff and vanished out of sight. After a few minutes they heard the rabbit feet thumping that always gives excitement and makes you forget about the freezing cold.

The dogs were now ready to pounce and they expected a result. Five minutes went by and the ferret showed at one of the holes. It then turned back and vanished again. They waited a while longer but nothing happened.

Dad took the other ferret out and placed it by a hole. It went straight in and within thirty seconds a rabbit shot out of another hole and was trapped in a net. Dad fought off Digger and Bruce and claimed it. There were no more rabbits in that warren and the other warrens they tried seemed to be void of rabbits too.

There was a railway embankment at the side of the fields that had lots of rabbit burrows in it. Kenny did not have permission to ferret the railway embankment but they decided that no one would mind. A case of the other man's grass is greener.

They had no sooner started to set the nets when a train went past heading for Luton Station. They held the dogs as it passed to prevent any accidents and thought no more about it. It was about thirty minutes later when they were netting up a large warren when the fun started. The dogs had disappeared down a couple of large holes when dad suddenly noticed some movement behind him. He looked around and just thirty yards away was a policeman with an aggressive looking German Shepherd heading across the field towards them. Kenny said, 'I think we are in trouble now.' and started to grin. The policeman was soon at the other side of the wire fence at the bottom of the embankment with his dog straining at the lead. He said, 'Pick up your nets, you are on railway property and you are trespassing.' Dad's fearless terriers must have heard the strange voice because they both appeared together out of different holes. What happened next was hilarious. Digger and Bruce glanced at each other and as though it was a signal they then made a beeline for the German Shepherd, which immediately stopped pulling at the lead and leapt back slipping its collar. For the next few minutes it tore around the field with these two miniature terriers in pursuit with war cries screaming from their muzzles.

The policeman, who up to this point had seemed quite calm, started shouting at dad and Kenny to call the dogs in. Dad knew that would be a waste of breath so Kenny and dad started running after them, trying to catch them. It took about ten minutes to catch them but not before they had nipped the back legs of the German Shepherd several times, cleverly avoiding the German Shepherd's snapping teeth.

With all dogs back on their leads dad and Kenny were marched back across the fields. The policeman was not happy and as they were marching he was constantly informing them that they would pay dearly. It didn't improve matters when Kenny said, 'I thought police dogs were supposed to be aggressive.'

When they reached the truck on the grass verge they found that the police van was parked behind it. Dad put the dogs in the cab and the policeman obviously felt more confident now with the terriers out of the way. He told his dog to sit and then instructed both dad and Kenny to stand facing the cab of the truck with their hands outstretched above their heads. He then proceeded to frisk them just as a bus full of passengers went slowly past. Dad was thinking, I hope there are not any of my neighbours are on that bus, but before he had the chance to look, the two Jack Russells came out of the back window opening in the cab like lightning.

Within seconds they were in hot pursuit of the German Shepherd across the field again. Dad thought the policeman was going to explode and heard him cry out, 'Oh my God, not again!' He soon gave up the idea of frisking them and they were all in the field trying to catch the dogs. Dad felt sorry for the German Shepherd which looked petrified.

They did eventually catch the dogs and Kenny sat in the cab and held them. Not intending to take any more chances the policeman put his dog in the van. He then took dad and Kenny's details and confiscated the rabbit and the nets. The fact that they told him that they had caught the rabbit on the land where they had permission was of no consequence.

They eventually received a summons to appear before the Magistrates Court. The charge was, Trespassing in search of game.

A couple of days before the court case dad went down with a terrible dose of the flu. He rang the courthouse and informed them that he would be unable to attend.

Now, Kenny was a very shy sort of man and not good with words. If he couldn't sort his problems out with a good punch-up he always asked his wife to sort things for him. She spent most of her time running around after him. She even had to go to the doctor's for him when he was ill. Dad always reckoned that when Kenny died they would have his headstone inscribed with her name.

Anyway, he sent her to the court instead of going himself. When they called his name out she walked in and stipulated to the magistrate, 'My husband pleads guilty to trespassing but not in search of game, because it was a rabbit and he had caught it somewhere else.' The magistrate was quick to point out that it was all one charge and could not be split in two. He shook his head and adjourned the case to be held at a later date.

They never heard any more about it. Whether the rabbit, being the evidence, had gone rotten, or they gave it up as a bad job, not wanting to face Kenny's wife again, dad didn't know. But what he did learn was the other man's grass might be greener, but it can cause you a lot of problems.

The driver of the train had telephoned in to the station and the police had responded. I think the policeman will view Jack Russells slightly different after that episode.

After dad had told that story we left Tony's house. I don't remember much about the journey home but I know I enjoyed my dinner when we arrived. Dad seemed very pleased with me and I went to sleep that night feeling very contented and relieved to still be a virgin. I liked being in Grob's company but I am going to have to sit on it in the future when Tony isn't watching him. Pity about the stupid hare.

CHAPTER 3

Trials and Trivialization

During the Summer months we had spent time at some unofficial gundog trials. They were supposed to be not too serious but most people who entered their dogs took it very seriously indeed. Prior to the trials dad had spent a lot of time with me, making sure I would work with dummies and be obedient. I enjoyed the training and tried to please him. I particularly enjoyed swimming in the rivers while retrieving the dummies. I just love swimming.

The day finally arrived when I was entered into my first trial. I think dad was more nervous than I was. All the way there dad was talking to me saying, 'Just do your best Bess. It doesn't matter if we don't win.'

There were a lot of dogs there and I thought it would be a good place to get to know some of them, but their owners wouldn't let them mix with other dogs and just kept them on their own. It was all very serious and I couldn't understand what the big thing was about picking up dummies and bringing them back.

Amongst the many competitors and spectators were a few others that shoot with dad throughout the season. Dad had become very friendly with a man there called Harry. He had a yellow Labrador called Sheba who was not at all impressed with the trials. She said to me, 'What pleasure can they possibly get from sending us out to fetch a stuffed green bag with a bit of rope sewn on the end of it?' I replied, 'I suppose it is better than lying around at home doing nothing.' She smiled and said, 'You speak for yourself Bess, I quite like lying around at home doing nothing. I think this is so boring, and have you noticed how they always find an area of long grass to throw the dummy into. When we go in to retrieve it we stir up all the flies that are on the grass and they inevitably have a meal from us. I have been virtually eaten alive at some of these trials and I do not like it. When the flies start biting them they rub repellent on themselves but they never worry about us, do they?'

Dad and I did not have a good day at our first trial. When dad saw the four judges he said to Harry, 'This will be a waste of time! Two of those judges dislike me. I told them a few home truths about gun safety one day on a shoot and they have never forgotten me. One of them was passing a closed gun over a fence to the other, and believe it or not the man he was passing it to took hold of it by the barrels which were pointing at him. They may know something about dog training but they are certainly ignorant when it comes to gun safety.'

There were four tests to compete in and a maximum of twenty points were awarded on each test. Every time a mistake was made points were deducted.

The first test I found quite easy. I had a blind retrieve to find but I had a good idea where it should be. I set off in the direction where dad pointed and worked slowly out. When dad blew his stop whistle I stopped and turned to face him. He signalled for me to go to the right and I soon smelt the scent. I retrieved the dummy from under some bushes and brought it back to him and presented it nicely. Dad was delighted when we were given maximum points.

The next test is where it started to go wrong. The judge stood on a path in a wood and we had to go and stand next to him. He said to dad, 'Tell your dog to sit and then you will hear a shot. A dummy will be thrown from out of the wood and you will see it land in the bracken. Send your dog when I tell you.' A shot was fired and I was waiting to see the dummy come out. It was supposed to have been thrown high enough for me to see it but it must have slipped out of the thrower's hand and stayed very low. Dad must have thought I had seen it being thrown because he sent me out. I decided to keep going out until he stopped me and then he could give me a clue as to where it was with some signals. I had gone out quite a way when I looked back in time to see him fumbling with his whistle trying to get it into his mouth. He eventually blew it and I stopped. I had a good sniff and smelt the scent of a dummy. I set off in the direction of the scent and soon found that there were two dummies lying side by side at a man's feet at the edge of the wood. I picked one up and took it back to dad. I lost ten points for that retrieve, because it was not the dummy I was supposed to fetch. The one that I had brought back was a spare one that the dummy thrower had left on the ground. Dad was not pleased with me but it was his fault. He must have been dreaming when I was running out. All he had to do was blow his whistle to stop me but he never even had it in his mouth. Dad said to me, 'Bloody marvellous! We are ten points down and the next two tests are the judges that don't like me.'

The third test was a water test with two retrieves. The dog that ran before me had failed on the second retrieve and the dummy was floating away down the river. The judge said to dad, 'Could you send your dog for that one.' Dad sent me and I brought it back. I then had my own two dummies to retrieve and I had no problems with either of them. The judge deducted three points anyway as dad had expected.

The fourth test was a straight forward retrieve but a long way. The starting pistol was fired and the dummy was launched. I saw it and I knew where it would be. I had to sit for a minute and then dad sent me. I was just ten yards from the dummy when a black flatcoat ran across from the side and picked it up. He then ran off back to his owner with it, who was in the spectator area. Dad whistled for me to come in and I did. The judge said to dad, 'You can run her again if you want, although she was a bit slow,' to which dad replied, 'No I don't think so. I have had enough for one day and you will deduct points regardless.' He then said, 'Come on Bess,' and we walked back to the car park.

Harry was already there and asked, 'How did you get on Vince?' dad replied, 'As expected,' Harry then said, 'I noticed that the judge on the water test has brought his son here today and he has entered a Labrador with a head on it like a horse.' Dad replied, 'There is only one winner today then. That pair of judges are bloody cheats.'

We watched some of the other competitors perform and there were some pretty good dogs there. There were also some dogs who didn't have a clue but seemed to enjoy it anyway. When the big headed Labrador took the water test he made a complete mess of it. A dummy was launched from the opposite bank and the dog was sent for it. While he was swimming back with it another dummy was launched from the same place. Instead of taking the first dummy to his handler and then returning to the water for the second he turned around and swam back for the second one with the first one still in his mouth. He managed to get hold of it without dropping the first one and swam back with them both in his mouth. The dog was so pleased with the retrieves he didn't want to part with them and kept running around the handler, who was the judge's son. Eventually the handler grabbed the dummies and pulled them out of the dog's mouth. The dog was excited and decided to go in the water again and have another search. He came back after a lot of whistle blowing and shouting and was put on a lead. The judge deducted just one point for that performance. I am sure it would have been maximum if we hadn't been watching. Dad said, 'They should hang that judge from the tree that he is standing under.' A bit harsh, I thought, but I knew what he meant. If only dad wouldn't take it so serious. After all, they are only dummies and we are supposed to enjoy it.

All the competitors had now completed the tests and the cards had been handed in to a couple of men in a caravan. They were going to add the scores up and declare the winners. Meanwhile there was a scurry going on. We stood and watched for a while and it looked great fun. A dummy was thrown and the dog had to sit until the handler sent it. As soon as the dog was sent a stopwatch was started and when the dog came back to the handler with the dummy the stopwatch was stopped and the time recorded. There was a prize for the fastest dog. Dad said to me, 'You can run a bit Bess. I think we will have a go at this.'

When it came to our turn dad asked the man with the stopwatch, 'What is the best time so far?' The man replied, 'Twelve and a half seconds.' The dummy was thrown and I heard dad say, 'Get on!' I ran out as fast as I could. I picked the dummy up and ran back to him. He took it off me and the man clicked his stopwatch and said, 'You are in the lead! That was twelve seconds exactly.'

We watched several other dogs but none of them were very fast. When we thought it was all over the man who had been judging the water test said, 'I think I will have a go now.' He went over to his car and let a Labrador out of the back. Dad said, 'I have seen that dog on some shoots. It is useless apart from the fact it can run. He must have brought it especially for the scurry.'

The dummy was thrown and the dog was sent. The dog collected the dummy and as he was running back with it his handler took five paces backwards. The dog came running flat out and when it crossed the line the man stopped the stopwatch. He then looked at it and said, 'You have won! It was eleven and three-quarter seconds.'

Dad was standing close by and said to the man with the stopwatch, 'You stopped the watch before the dog gave the dummy to his handler.' He replied, 'That's okay! I stopped the watch when the dog crossed over the line.' Dad said, 'But my dog had to slow down to give me the dummy, that man took five steps backwards.' He replied, You can do that if you want to.' To which dad said, 'Okay I will run again.' 'Sorry' was the reply, 'Only one go each.'

Dad was fuming. He said, 'You lot are cheating bastards.' The man replied, 'You are a bad loser.' Dad said, 'You are wrong mate. I am not a bad loser but me and my dog have put a lot of work into the training before we came here, but you bastards have it rigged before it even starts.' He went on to say, 'Let's go over to the caravan and see who has won today, and if it isn't the judge's son's dog who is declared the winner I will give you five pounds.'

Everybody collected in front of the caravan and the prizes were presented. The winner of the day was the dog with the horse's head. Dad turned around to the man with the stopwatch and said, 'I knew my five pounds was safe, just as I knew the five pounds I paid to enter was wasted.'

We then went home and he moaned to mum about it all evening. I was beginning to regret the day they ever invented dummies. Whatever did he mean when he said, Just do your best Bess. It doesn't matter if we don't win.

CHAPTER 4

First day beating

I knew dad wasn't getting ready to go to work because he was far too happy. I was becoming quite excited as I thought we were going to go shooting. Well, he took his shooting jacket out of the cupboard, mum prepared the packed lunch and everything was going like normal. But when we left the house and walked to the car he didn't have his gun with him. I know he can be very forgetful sometimes, having been out with him on the foreshore. On one occasion we had walked out nearly a mile onto the mud when he realised that he had left his gun in the car. He was really grumpy as we were going back for it and having a go at me as though it was my fault. He causes no end of problems for himself but whoever is the closest to him at the time generally gets the blame.

This time I tried to tell him by going back to the house door and sitting there. I was saying, 'You have forgotten your gun.' But it is strange how humans can't hear us dogs talk. He looked at me sitting at the door and said, 'Get in the car or I will leave you behind you stupid dog.' Me stupid! That's good coming from him. Anyway I decided to get in and we were soon on our way.

After a long drive on some roads that I hadn't been on before we turned on to a track that ran through a forest. The track was full of potholes and dad cursed every time a wheel dropped into a hole and the bottom of the car hit the track. He muttered, 'Bloody ridiculous! You get paid ten pounds for the day and do one hundred pounds worth of damage to the car trying to get there.' I didn't know what he was talking about at the time but that was nothing unusual. He comes out with all kinds of rubbish that I don't understand. I decided to just look out of the window and ignore him.

I was quite amazed at the number of pheasants I saw. They were all over the place and dad had to stop the car a couple of times so as not to run over them. I was hoping he would let me out and I would have moved them for him but instead he opened his window and started shouting at them. A fat lot of good that did so he started to drive slowly towards them. I was waiting for the bump as the car wheels ran over them but they must have dived out of the way at the last minute. All these pheasants and the idiot has forgotten his gun.

A ninety-degree turn in the track took us into a farmyard, which had a house and lots of outbuildings built around it. There were half a dozen cars of different shapes and colours parked in various places and quite a lot of activity with people and dogs. Small groups of men were talking while their dogs were tearing around emptying their bowels all over the place.

Dad got out of the car and wandered across to one of the groups. As one of the men turned around I noticed it was Tony. The fact that he was rolling a cigarette helped me to recognise him. From behind one of the buildings came another face I knew. It was Grob. He saw dad and looked across towards the car. I had moved onto the driving seat by now and was looking out of the window that dad had left open. Grob came tearing across, altering course on the way to make sure he had gone through the deepest muddy puddle before planting both his front paws on the side of dad's car and sticking his head in the open window. He said, 'Hello darling. I was hoping you would be here.' I said, 'You are not having my body Grob so don't even try.' He replied, 'As if I would.' Just in time to receive a crack around his ear from Tony. I heard Grob's nails dig in to the paint of the car door as he slid down. When dad came over he was nearly in tears looking at Grob's handiwork. 'Look what he has done,' dad moaned to Tony. Tony stood there looking at the car door for a second. He then shrugged his shoulders and pulled his tobacco tin out and rolled another cigarette, in a way that only he can.

Dad opened the door and I jumped out. He was more interested in his car door than me and I wandered over to some of the other dogs to see if there were any there that I knew. There were a lot of dogs there that I had never met. A mixture of all shapes and sizes and they all seemed desperate to check out the smell of each other's bum.

I looked around just in time to see Grob approaching with an eager look and I sat immediately. 'Do you know these other dogs Grob?' I asked. He replied, 'Oh yes. I have been out with this lot a few times. I will tell you all about them during the day.' I then said, 'Dad has forgotten his gun and hasn't realised it yet, and it looks as though all these other men have too.' Grob replied, 'They are not shooting today Bess, they are beating.' 'What is beating?' I enquired. 'Well,' Grob replied, 'It's a bit like slavery really. The posh people will be shooting and we will all be their slaves for the day. The good thing is we will get to flush out a lot of pheasants.' 'Will we get a retrieve?' I asked. 'Only if we are lucky,' Grob replied, 'There will be other people with dogs to do the picking-up. They are a weird bunch of blokes and women who think their dogs are wonderful, but some of them are crap.' 'Well why do they let them do it?' I asked. Grob looked at me and replied, 'It is just the way it is Bess. The working class do the beating. The middle class do the picking-up and the upper crust do the shooting. I don't know why but that's how it is. Don't you worry your pretty head about it and try and stay close to me. I will show you how to enjoy the day.'

Moments later a tractor which was pulling a trailer came from the track and turned into the farmyard. At the same time a man came out of the house. He was a huge man who had squeezed into a tweed suit that had probably been made for him when he was four stone lighter. His face was covered in hair, which I suppose could have been a beard but it looked more like a pubic disaster. Grob said, 'Look out! Here comes Hardy the keeper. He does a lot of shouting but most of us ignore him anyway. Laurel won't be far behind him.' A young man who was the under-keeper came out next. It was hard to define how old he might have been because he was so thin and he looked as though he hadn't eaten a decent meal for a long time.

Hardy looked around at his motley bunch of men and dogs and bellowed, 'Get in the trailer. We are going!' Grob said, 'Follow me Bess. We don't want to be last in or you spend most of the time hanging out the back.' There was a bit of a scramble and we all started to pile into the trailer. It had a canvas cover over it and several bales of straw down each side and across the front. It was probably suitable for ten people but today there were sixteen men and eighteen dogs. Somehow we all managed to get in and as the tractor set off three nearly fell out of the back. Laurel and Hardy were travelling in front of the tractor in Hardy's Landrover.

Well, this trailer had been built long before the days of suspension and when a wheel dropped into the first pothole half of the men fell off the bales and landed on top of the dogs, which were stacked three high anyway. By the time we had reached the bottom of the track there were bodies all over the place and it looked as though all the men and the dogs had been put into a bowl and given a quick whirl by an electric mixer. Once we were onto the smooth road everyone managed to sort themselves out and the dogs found their rightful owners. It was the start of the day and everyone was in a good mood, but that was going to change as the day progressed.

The tractor stopped suddenly and the whole pile of man and dog flesh heaved towards the front. I heard dad moan as a twenty-six stone geriatric beater landed on his foot. Hardy was now stood outside the rear of the trailer. The men that were sitting at the rear started to get out but Hardy was quick to shout at them, 'Get out when I tell you!' He then shouted, 'Where is Big Jimmy?' A voice from beneath three others at the front of the trailer replied with a muffled mutter, 'I am in here.' Hardy shouted, 'Well get yourself out here, I want you on the flush line with the under-keeper.' Well, it was like trying to squeeze a cork out of a wine bottle but somehow, with much shoving and pushing, not to mention a fair bit of groaning, Big Jimmy managed to eject himself from the mass. Hardy gave Laurel a two-way radio and said to him, 'Take Big Jimmy to the flush line and use the radio to let me know when the guns are in position.' Laurel managed to summon up enough energy to grunt an acknowledgement and went off with Big Jimmy in the Landrover.

In the meantime one of the men had managed to release a packet of cigarettes from his top pocket and handed them round. Five of them lit up and within seconds the small amount of clean air that we had under the canvas cover was filled with smoke. I started coughing and within minutes so were most of the other dogs and half of the men.

Hardy finally gave the orders for us to get out of the trailer and we all emerged. Tony stated, 'Fresh air at last!' And started to roll another cigarette.

Hardy had the other two-way radio in his hand and he was vigorously shaking it and then holding it to his ear. The radio kept crackling and making screeching noises. He put the radio to his mouth and shouted into it, 'Is that you there?' There was a pause but no reply. He then said, 'Will you bloody well answer me, you prat?' After listening to a few more screeches coming out of the speaker Hardy started cursing.

While all this was going on I noticed that a rather handsome looking black Labrador dog was eyeing me up and down. I smiled at him and he started to walk over towards me. He had only travelled a few yards when his master gave him a hell of a whack with his stick. I saw the poor dog's face wince from the pain of the blow and he scuttled back to stand behind his master again. I looked up at dad and he was in deep conversation with two other beaters so I went across to see the Labrador. I said to him, 'I bet that hurt.' He replied, 'Yes it damn well did. He is always doing that to me. One day I will sink my teeth into his leg. Anyway, I haven't seen you here before. What is your name?' I replied, 'My name is Bess and this is my first time beating.' He then said, 'They call me Jet and I have been coming here for three years. You stick close to me Bess and I will show you the ropes.' I said, 'Thanks Jet, I might just do that.' Grob must have spotted us and was becoming jealous, because he came over with the hair on his back sticking upright and he was definitely looking for trouble. Jet stepped forward to meet the aggressor and almost immediately received another mighty blow from his master's stick. Jet winced again and Grob took one look and decided against any further action in case he got some of the same treatment.

Hardy announced that the two-way radio was a load of tat, and that if the guns were not in place by now it was tough luck. The next order was, 'Follow me,' and he set off at a fast pace. The order came as a bit of a surprise and most of the beaters found themselves running to catch up with him. He took us to the beginning of a large wood and told the beaters to line out. They all lined out along the edge of the wood about twenty-five yards apart. Dad told me to stay at heel so that is what I was doing. Jet was three beaters away on my right and he was sitting behind his master but looking at me. I smiled at him and he smiled back. Grob was four beaters away to my left and he was watching me as well.

The next order was, 'Let's go!' Dad lifted me over the wire fence and then climbed over it himself. We walked into the wood and slowly forward. Hardy was shouting orders to keep in a straight line and keep your dogs in and dad was tapping the trees with his stick as he walked past them. There were a few dogs tearing about on my left and their owners were shouting at them to come in. The next thing that happened was a lot of pheasants taking to the air where these dogs were. Hardy bellowed, 'Get those bloody dogs back in.' A man ran forward out of the line and grabbed his spaniel by the back of the neck and then whacked it three times with his stick across its back. The dog yelled out with the pain and then followed his master back to the line of beaters.

Once more we set off walking and soon came to a big clearing with long grass. Dad told me to get on. I ran out about ten yards and then dad whistled for me to stop. I stopped and turned to look at him. He then signalled for me to quarter. I started quartering and there was lots of strong scent. After just a minute two pheasants broke cover in front of me. I heard dad say, 'Good girl,' so I carried on hunting. I could smell another very close and as I stuck my nose into a clump of grass a big cock bird ran out from the other side and took off like

Concorde. Another, 'Good girl,' call from dad and then the West Highland terrier on my right said mockingly, 'Who is a good girl then, the-noo?' I was a bit embarrassed and was hoping that dad would now keep his mouth shut. I flushed another six pheasants out of the clearing and every time the West Highland terrier on my right said, 'Who is a good girl then, the-noo?' I decided to ignore him and could now hear the guns firing in the distance. Hardy shouted. 'Wonderful! The guns have woken up at last.'

We came to the edge of the clearing and back into woodland. This was much more open than the previous wood with not so much cover. I could see well ahead and there were a lot of pheasants in a bunch just stood looking at us as we approached. Hardy ordered, 'Steady now, we don't want them all out together.' Just as he said that a hare got up in front of me. Dad instinctively shouted, 'No!' I wasn't going to chase it anyway but there was a very leggy spaniel next to me and he had different ideas. He went off like a greyhound straight after the hare leaving his master screaming obscenities. Within seconds the hare and the dog were into the bunch of pheasants, which flew up in all directions. To say that Hardy was annoyed would be the understatement of the year. I thought he was going to blow a gasket.

The line had stopped and a few minutes later the spaniel returned looking rather pleased with himself and wondering why everyone had stopped. He soon got the message when he was within range of the stick. That was the third dog to get a hiding and we were only halfway through the first drive. I was beginning to understand why they call it "beating."

We started walking again and the further we went the more pheasants seemed to accumulate in front of us. I was at heel now, as were most of the dogs. There were a few dogs who didn't seem to know what heel was and they were now on leads. The birds were flying up over the trees and across a valley where the guns were blasting away at them. We moved forward another twenty yards and I could now see Laurel and Big Jimmy. There was one on each end of a rope which was spread across a clearing in the wood. The rope had pieces of plastic hanging on it and Laurel and Big Jimmy were waving it up and down. The pheasants were keeping well away from the rope and we were closing in on them. Hardy shouted, 'Hold it there and just tap your sticks.' We all stopped and the men started to tap their sticks on the trees and on their boots. The pheasants started to walk around in circles, looking at each other as though they were hoping that one of them knew a safe way out of there. Every few minutes a dozen or so would panic and take to the air and the guns would blast away again.

When there were just a few pheasants left Hardy gave the order, 'Put your dogs in.' Within seconds a dozen dogs were tearing around and the rest of the pheasants flew out of the wood. Dad never told me to go so I had to sit and watch. The leggy spaniel who had been next to me was having a wonderful time and I would have liked to have had a go myself. Hardy blew a whistle and that was the signal for the end of the drive.

We walked to the edge of the wood and I could now see the guns and the others who do the picking-up. There was a man picking-up with two yellow Labradors. Well, one was trying to pick-up but the other was just running into it, almost knocking it off its feet. It was just a puppy that wanted to play and I heard dad saying that it was far too young to be there.

One of the guns must have had a good stand because there were about twenty dead pheasants lying on the ground within a fifty-yard circle around him. The man just put his gun in its slip and nonchalantly walked away from the carnage without even looking at the birds, as much as to say. 'Nothing to do with me!'

We stood and watched for a while as the picking-up dogs were working and then it was time to go. All the beaters had formed into little groups and were walking across some fields heading back to the slavery trailer. Nobody seemed to mind now what the dogs were doing so most of us took the opportunity to stretch our legs a bit.

I was running at an easy pace when Jet came alongside me. 'What did you think to that Bess?' he asked. I said, 'I really enjoyed it but I don't think that spaniel next to me did. Did you see the battering he got?' Jet replied, 'The dog's name is Sammy but he is a bit on the thick side. Every time he comes here he does the same thing and chases after the hares. Every time he comes back he gets a belting from his dad. You would think he would either stop chasing the things, or at least if he had chased one, then he would have enough sense not to come back for a while.' He went on to say, 'I blame his dad though. He knows what Sammy will do but he never puts him on the lead. Time after time he lets Sammy mess the drive up. I don't know why Hardy lets them come. But there again, I don't think Hardy has any more sense than Sammy anyway.' I asked, 'What do we do now Jet?' He replied, 'We do another drive before lunch and then two after. The next drive is much better than the first one because the cover is a lot thicker and your dad won't be able to see you all the time. When we start the drive I will pop over and we can sneak off and enjoy ourselves.' There was then a loud voice shouting, 'Jet, get in here.' Jet said, 'The old bastard's off again but I will see you later.' He then ran off.

He had no sooner gone than I felt Grob's cold nose around my loins. I quickly sat again. 'What did that flash bastard want?' He asked. I said, 'Oh nothing Grob. Just passing the time of day.' Grob said, 'You want to watch him Bess. He is only after one thing you know.' I replied, 'Would that be the same thing that you are after Grob?' He sort of screwed up his face as though he couldn't deny it and then replied, 'But that's different Bess, I am your friend.' I said, 'Well, you won't be my friend much longer if you keep sticking your cold nose in my private bits.' Grob smiled and replied, 'Point taken.' He then ran off after a flatcoat that had a definite scent indicating that it was just starting to come into season. The flatcoat turned and snapped at Grob with a set of choppers that an alligator would have been proud of. Grob cleverly moved his head in time. He turned to me and grinned and then ran off to annoy some other dog that was minding its own business.

We were all stacked back in the trailer and ready to go to the next drive. It went quiet for a few seconds and then the West Highland terrier said mockingly, 'Who is a good girl then, the-noo?' I started to blush with embarrassment and then Jet said, 'Shut your mouth Jock. At least Bess can work and that's more than can be said for you.' The reply was, 'Och Bess, I think someone fancies you, you ken.' Jet retorted quite angrily, 'I fancy taking a lump out of your ear you short legged Scottish tosser.' Grob stuck his nose in and said, 'What's all the noise about?' Jet replied, 'Mind your own business Grob or you will get the same,' Grob wasn't used to being spoken to like that and responded in the only way he knew how, by leaping forward and latching on to one of Jet's front legs. Jet grabbed a mouthful of Grob's ear and for a few moments it was total chaos in the trailer. The twenty-six stone geriatric beater tried to get out of the way because most of the action was taking place between his legs. Of course there wasn't really anywhere to go and he came to rest on the flatcoat's tail. She let out a yelp and poor Sammy, who was unfortunate enough to be within striking distance of the choppers, got the blame. Sammy howled after receiving an alligator type bite and then a couple of the beaters managed to get some order back in the trailer by belting a few innocent dogs with their sticks. Jock had caused all the bother but he came out of it unscathed. Some of the beaters started arguing with each other and the tension was mounting. Then someone in their wisdom decided that it would be a good idea if they all had a smoke and the smog came in again. The mixture of sweaty men, steaming dogs and choking smoke was something else.

Hardy's Landrover stopped and the tractor stopped behind it. Before Hardy had managed to walk to the back of the trailer to tell us to stay put, ninety percent of us were out. Hardy shouted, ' What is the matter with you lot today? I only want two out here to cover the flanks.' Big Jimmy and Geriatric were given the job and the rest of us filed back into the gas chamber and we were off again.

The tractor pulled off the road into a field and then stopped. Nobody moved this time and Hardy came to the back of the trailer with Laurel. He shouted, 'Move up we are coming in.' Laurel had no trouble in squeezing his pencil-like body in, but Hardy couldn't find anywhere to sit and just stood at the rear with his back to us. He bellowed to the tractor driver. 'Okay.' The tractor set off across the bumpy field and Hardy was hanging on to the metal frame, which supported the canvas cover. Just when I thought things couldn't get any worse Hardy broke wind and nearly choked us all. There were screams from the beaters of, 'You dirty bastard.' But Hardy thought it was hilarious and roared with laughter. I looked at Laurel and couldn't decide whether he was dead or not.

After several more reports from Hardy's rear end the tractor stopped and we all jumped out. Jet said to me, 'I will see you later.' Then we all formed a line at the beginning of something that I can only describe as a wilderness. It had obviously been a wood at some time but now there were more trees lying than standing. There was a mixture of grass and bramble about four feet high which covered the ground between the trees. Hardy shouted, 'Let's go and let your dogs work.' The line of beaters started to move slowly forward and I received the instruction to get on. Dad was struggling to make any headway through the jungle but I found that underneath there were lots of runs that must have been formed by the wild animals and birds. It would be difficult to put your head up through the canopy but no problem at all running around below it.

There were a few pheasants in there that would rather run than fly but occasionally one would break through the canopy, usually followed out by the head of an over zealous spaniel with a mouthful of tail feathers.

I had been working for a while when Jet came running up. He said, 'Follow me Bess and I will show you where the real action is.'

'What about my dad?' I asked, ' He will be angry if I run off.' Jet replied, 'Don't worry about your dad. He can't see you in here and he won't even know you are gone. Anyway, we will only be five minutes.'

He set off through the ready-made runs and I decided to follow him. We were heading down to the end of the line of beaters and passed several dogs working on our way. When we came to the end of the line Jet said, 'There is a ditch over there that runs down the side of the wood. It will be loaded with pheasants hiding from the beaters. Hardy knows that there will be a lot of birds in there but he also knows that if he leaves the ditch alone there will be plenty of birds left for the next time they work this wood.' I said, 'Perhaps we should leave them then.' Jet started laughing and said, 'Be wise Bess. Where is your sense of adventure? Let's get in there and shift them anyway.'

He ran into the ditch and I followed him. There was some water in the bottom and brambles growing up each side. He said, 'You take this side and I will take the other.' We started hunting the brambles and almost immediately pheasants started breaking out. I was really enjoying myself flushing birds every few seconds. The guns were very busy now and we must have flushed two hundred birds when Jet said, 'That was great fun Bess but I think we should get back now.' We made our way back to the beaters' line and then I could hear dad's whistle calling me in. I said to Jet, 'I did enjoy it but I will be in deep trouble now.' He replied, 'No you won't Bess. Just keep under cover and creep up behind him. He will never know you have been far away.' I did as he said and came out behind dad who was still blowing his whistle. I gave a little whine as though I was trying to tell him I had been there for ages. He turned and saw me. 'Oh there you are!' he said, 'I thought I had lost you in the undergrowth.' I just wagged my tail and he bent down and stroked me. I didn't realise how easy it was to do your own thing and get away with it. That Jet is some dog. I think I am beginning to fall for him.

We finished the drive but Hardy was not at all happy. The beater who had been on the end of the line working about thirty yards away from the ditch at the side of the wood was an ugly looking specimen. He had an enormous nose, which was a sort of red and purple blotchy colour. He had a cross spaniel-Labrador bitch with him but she was a miserable dog. She was reluctant to speak to the rest of us and she hated working. She seemed to be very conscious about her appearance and every time she got a bit of dirt on her coat she stopped to lick it off.

Hardy said to the man, 'I thought I had told you not to let your dog hunt in the ditch.' Rudolf replied indignantly, 'I didn't.' Hardy was looking really angry now and said, 'Like hell you didn't. I saw the birds coming out in their droves.' 'Well it wasn't my bloody dog in there.' replied Rudolf, and his nose seemed to turn more purple. 'It must have been your dog.' insisted Hardy, whose voice was getting louder. Rudolf stood still for a moment wondering what to say next. He then kicked his dog twice and called it an effing bastard, and that was the end of that episode. I was sitting next to Jet as this was going on and we couldn't contain ourselves. Jet said. 'If Hardy had half a brain he would have realised it couldn't have been Rudolf's dog in the ditch. She wouldn't want to get her feet wet.' I laughed until my tummy hurt.

The slavery wagon took us back to the farmyard for the lunch break and we all had another good shaking on the way. The beaters were not as happy as they had been earlier and they were grumbling amongst themselves.

They had their lunch in a big deserted barn. Hanging from the roof beams were one-hundred-year-old cobwebs that looked like lace curtains, and the place was filthy. They were sitting around a large table that was covered with bird droppings, with some fresher than others. Some of the dogs had been put in the cars but others were allowed into the barn. There was a good fire burning in the open grate and after I had scrounged some food from dad I lay down in front of the fire with the other dogs. I closed my eyes and thought of those pheasants in the ditch as I dozed off.

Grob woke me with a lick on the nose. He said, 'Are you trying to avoid me Bess?' Not wanting to hurt his feelings I said, 'Of course not Grob.' He then said, 'What's going on between you and Jet?' I said, 'Nothing as far as I am concerned.' But I was beginning to wish that there was. Grob said, 'I will spend more time with you this afternoon.' 'All right,' I said, and closed my eyes again.

I was listening to the beaters discussing the morning drives. Rudolf was complaining bitterly about his unfair treatment when dad said to him, 'Well, it's your own fault. You should have kept more control over your dog.' Rudolf said, 'Don't you start Vince. I suppose your dog is a little angel?' 'Well at least she doesn't run away and get me into trouble,' dad replied. I started to grin and thought of Jet.

When we went outside for the afternoon drives the weather had changed dramatically. It was pouring with rain and the wind had picked up. The beaters put on their waterproof clothing but of course us dogs don't have that privilege. By the time we climbed into the slave transporter I was wet. I had been lying in front of a roaring fire for an hour but the rain had soon got through my coat and I started to shiver. Jet saw me and said, 'Come and lay over here between me and the straw bales and I will keep you warm.' I did what he suggested and tucked in close to him. I didn't know what was happening but I was getting a very strange feeling in my tummy, and when Jet kissed me gently my whole body shuddered. I looked up to see where Grob was, expecting a reaction from him. Poor Grob had ended up at the back of the trailer and was fully occupied just trying not to fall out. I smiled at Jet and snuggled up again.

The trailer stopped and nobody rushed to get out. It was pretty cramped in there but at least it gave some shelter from the rain. Hardy was soon at the back shouting his orders. He said, 'The bloody guns are useless and they only shot eighty birds this morning. Somehow they have to shoot another one hundred and twenty this afternoon. We had better try and make them easy for them.' That was followed by, 'Come on. Everyone out!' The beaters reluctantly started climbing out and dad pulled the hood up on his coat.

The drive was a wood which Hardy rudely described as a dog's leg. There was a strip of rushes that were about fifty yards wide running alongside the edge of the wood and Hardy gave the job of working them to dad and Tony. Jet was taken to the other side of the wood and Grob was delighted that we would be working together. Hardy gave the order and we started.

I was working the strip next to the wood and Grob was on the outside of me. Grob and I had our work cut out working the rushes. There were plenty of birds in them but they were very reluctant to fly. They just sat tight and refused to move until you pushed your nose up their bums. Occasionally a pheasant would fly out of the wood in front of the beaters but I could see that most of the birds in the wood were just running along in front.

We were halfway along and turned with the dog's leg in the wood working down towards the end. Sometimes I met Grob in the middle of the rushes and on one occasion he said, 'This is better away from those other dogs Bess, with just you and me working together.' In a way he was right. He could be a bit boisterous but at least he didn't make fun of me like Jock did.

The pheasants in the wood had kept running forward and now there were a lot of birds in a group between the beaters and the flush line. Hardy stopped the line of beaters and signalled for Tony to work his way down on the outside of the wood to stop the birds breaking out the side. As Tony was walking down a big roe buck jumped up in front of Grob. The deer went on a panic run towards the wood, leaping over the fence at the edge of the wood and then straight into the gathering of pheasants. Well, some of the pheasants ran but most of them got up together and three-quarters of those flew back over the beaters. There were screams from Hardy of, 'Wave your arms!' and although the beaters were waving arms and sticks and making all kinds of noises the birds took absolutely no notice and flew to safety behind the line of beaters. Hardy stood there with his head in his hands and I thought he was going to cry. To make things worse the rain was now coming down in sheets. Hardy managed to pull himself together and the line carried on slowly forward.

The rushes had finished now and we were on a field of grass and had been ordered to stop. Grob had come across and was sitting next to me. I could see some of the guns clearly and enjoyed watching the shooting. Grob said, 'If the guns couldn't hit the birds in the morning when it was dry and they were sober, they certainly are not going to this afternoon with all their waterproof clothing on and a few drinks inside them.' He was right and most of the birds flew over the guns without being touched.

There was a gun in front of me and a picker-up thirty yards behind him with two black Labrador dogs. They had massive heads and were nowhere near as good-looking as Jet. A cock pheasant came out of the wood quite high and flew straight over the gun. He missed it with his first shot but turned around and hit it with the second while it was above the man picking-up. The bird was stone dead but the momentum kept it going and it landed in a bush thirty yards further on. The man picking-up had his cap pulled down over his face and was more interested in keeping the rain out than doing his job and hadn't noticed it.

A few moments later the whistle went to signal the end of the drive. The man shooting put his gun in its slip and walked away. As he went he signalled to the man picking-up that there was a bird down behind him. Grob and I watched this man trying to work these two dogs. He didn't have a clue where the bird was and neither did they. Grob said, 'Look at that pair. They will never find it.' I asked, 'Can we go and get it?' Grob replied, 'Best not to Bess or we might be in trouble. The pickers-up can become really nasty if we show their dogs up.'

Five minutes went by and then Hardy walked out towards the man and shouted, 'Have you picked them all?' The man picking-up replied, 'All but one, but I think it is a strong runner.' Hardy then shouted, 'Better leave it then and go to the next drive with the guns.' The man called his dogs in and walked away in the direction that the guns had gone.

Hardy gave the orders for us to go and we walked across the field back towards the trailer. That is we all did except Grob. He sneaked back and retrieved the pheasant. While he was gone I took the chance to walk alongside Jet. Grob returned and proudly carried his prize back to the trailer. While he was carrying it his tail never stopped wagging.

You couldn't see a thing in the trailer because of the steam coming off the dogs and Grob never noticed that Jet and I were together again.

The last drive of the day was on more open ground, which had some steep slopes. The rain was still hammering down and the beaters did not look a happy bunch. Tony and Grob were working next to dad and I, as we worked our way through some rather sharp blackthorn bushes. Dad was saying to me, 'Get in there.' I wouldn't mind going into the bushes if there was something in there even though the thorns are very sharp, but I had had a good sniff and my nose told me that there was nothing in there at all. Dad started to get angry with me insisting that I went into the bushes. I did as I was told even though there was nothing in there and a sharp thorn cut me right along the side of my tummy. As I came out the other side with blood flowing Grob said, 'Don't be stupid Bess. There is no point in going in if there is nothing there. Just run around the bushes for a while. That's what I do.' I followed Grob's advice and dad was not pleased because I wouldn't go in.

We came to the end of that clump of blackthorns and into more open ground. Grob started to quarter but because dad was angry with me I wasn't allowed to, and he shouted at me to heel, and that is where I had to stay. Every now and then he would slip on the mud and I would jump away because I thought he was going to stand on me. Each time this happened he shouted at me to, heel.

We came to a very steep decline and as we started to go down it I received another order to heel. Seconds later dad was airborne. He slipped and lost his footing. His stick flew up in the air and so did his feet. He was doing somersaults and came to rest at the bottom of the decline with the help of a blackthorn bush. Grob shouted to me, 'He wanted you to stay at heel. How does he expect you to follow that?' We both rolled up with laughing, and apart from my little cuddle with Jet, that was definitely the highlight of the day.

Dad slowly stood up while cursing the luck of the Raw. He had several scratches on his face which were bleeding and he started dabbing them with his handkerchief. Grob said, 'He didn't seem to enjoy going into the blackthorn himself. Serves him right is what I say.' He then ran back over to Tony and started working again. I stayed fairly close to dad but not too close in case he decided to have another flight.

The drive was soon over and we were trundled back to the farmyard in the bone-shaker. I heard Hardy telling dad that the guns had only shot forty birds in the afternoon and they were complaining. As he was giving dad his ten pounds pay he said, 'At least you have got something out of the day Vince. There is no way I will get any tips from the guns today.' Dad replied. 'At least you haven't got a body covered in bruises, a scratched face and a damaged car.' Just before I got in the car Jet came over and said, 'Bye Bess, I hope I see you soon.' I replied, 'So do I Jet.'

When we arrived home Dad had a bath and did a lot of complaining to mum about his pains, but I agree with Grob. It did serve him right. I enjoyed my dinner that night and afterwards I climbed into my basket, licked myself clean and then slept like a log. I think I am going to enjoy this beating malarkey, and hopefully I will soon be seeing Jet again. He is gorgeous!

CHAPTER 5

The Ouse Washes

I will never forget my first wildfowling trip to the Ouse Washes. Dad had organised it and the party included dad and Tony and two others that had just joined the pheasant shooting syndicate which dad was in. One of them was known to dad as Disastrous Den and the other one was a bit of a snob called Charles. Disastrous Den had a springer spaniel called Lulu that never stopped talking and Charles had a Welsh spaniel called Henry that gave the impression that he thought that he was a station above the rest of us, very much like his dad. Grob soon gave Henry the name of Taffy, which we all adopted. Dad reckoned that Charles was a plastic millionaire, in as much as everything he owned was flashy and looked good. He wasn't concerned about quality, he was more concerned about show and impressing his friends.

Charles certainly seemed to be better off than the others and had recently bought a boat. After listening to dad and Tony talking about previous trips that they had been on to the Ouse Washes it is a wonder that they managed to live to tell their tales, considering some of the boats that they had risked their lives in. Charles had been on the telephone telling dad that they could use his new boat on the Hundred Foot River to get to the cabin on Pontoon Wash.

Early Sunday morning and we were getting ready to go. I didn't really know what was happening except that I knew it was something exciting by dad's mood. He had spent the previous day preparing everything. He had obtained some new camouflage netting and new hide poles. I heard him telling mum that the poles he had before were all bent from trying to push them into the ground so, although they were heavy, he had opted for solid steel poles this time and he had ground a sharp point on the end of them. They were the first thing to go on to the back of the pickup truck, closely followed by a bag of clothes, several bags of food. A plastic container with five gallons of drinking water in it, his gun and enough cartridges to wipe every bird off the face of the earth, a pair of thigh waders, a couple of coats and a small first aid kit. Oh yes, I nearly forgot. A litre bottle of whisky, which I have learnt over the years, is not only important, but also an absolutely essential part of any wildfowling expedition, regardless of the problems it generally causes.

A kiss for mum and we were on our way to collect Tony. Charles was collecting Disastrous Den and they were making their own way to the meeting place, which was in the car park of The Three Pickerels at Mepal, by the bridge over the Hundred Foot River. Dad was always talking about the times he had been wildfowling at Pontoon Wash on the Ouse Washes, and how they stayed in a log cabin which is built on stilts, and this is where we were heading.

When dad stopped the pickup truck Tony was sitting on a heap of gear at the gate outside his house. Grob was sitting next to him and I am sure he gets bigger each time I see him. Dad climbed out of the cab to help Tony load his stuff on the back of the truck, but in his usual manor Tony just kept sitting on it and took out his tobacco tin. Dad had to wait until Tony had rolled his cigarette and then they loaded his gear.

I looked out of the window at Grob and he was wagging his tail when he saw me. Dad opened the door and Grob jumped in. He said, 'Hi Bess, good to see you.' and went straight in for a sniff. He is so fussy and strong it took him about ten seconds to knock me off the seat and onto the floor. I said, 'Bugger me Grob! There is no need to knock me onto the floor. I smell just the same as I did the last time that you saw me.' He replied, 'Sorry Bess! I didn't mean to. Get back up here and I will behave myself.' I climbed back on the seat and he roughly licked my face. I don't think the word gentle is in Grob's vocabulary.

Dad and Tony climbed in and there was not much room in the cab. Tony resolved the problem by putting me on his knee and Grob took the centre seat. Tony said, 'You sit still Grobally or I will put you on the back.' Grob just gave him one of his looks and said to me, 'He has been nasty to me this morning and all I was doing was trying to help.' 'What happened?' I asked. Grob went on to say, 'Well, when I was in the garden this morning I noticed that there was a mole working away under the lawn. The molehill was growing as I was watching it. I decided to catch the offender and dug a big hole while trying. Unfortunately, I was within inches of catching it when he came out and saw my back end sticking out of his precious lawn. If it hadn't been for my mum I think he would have shot me there and then. No matter how I try I can't seem to please him.' I said, 'I don't think you try very hard Grob.' He replied, 'Bloody right I don't,' and we both started laughing. I was looking forward to this new adventure. I knew Grob and I would have a laugh if nothing else.

When we pulled into The Pickerels car park they were there waiting. The car, which belonged to Charles, was gleaming and it had a trailer hitched behind with a small boat on it. The most noticeable thing was that Charles had a big lumpy type of spot on the end of his nose, which looked crusty. Dad said quietly to Disastrous Den, 'What's wrong with Charles's nose, is it an extra sight to improve his shooting?' Den grinned and quietly replied, 'It's a wart that has recently grown, but don't mention it. He is very conscious of it and gets upset when anyone talks about it.'

Tony and dad started to examine the boat. It was about six feet long and four feet wide at the blunt end. It looked as though it had been constructed with plastic and had come out of a mould, with the hull being extremely thin. Charles wasn't worried about the quality and had a smile on his face while he was savouring the moment of everyone looking at his boat. Tony said, 'Charlie, how many people do you think you are going to get into that before it sinks? I have seen bigger washing-up bowls.' Half the smile quickly vanished as he replied, 'My name isn't Charlie, it is Charles, and I was assured when I purchased this boat that it was stable and seaworthy.' Tony walked around the other side of the boat and asked, 'Have you tested it yet?' Charles sort of hesitated and then replied with a drawn out, 'Nooo.'

Tony stood looking at the boat while taking out his tobacco tin and he slowly rolled a cone shaped cigarette. After lighting it and smoking it halfway down with his first draw he shrugged his shoulders and said, 'I will walk to the cabin Charlie.' Dad quickly added, 'I think I will too.' Charles had now lost the smile completely and said, 'You can please yourselves! I will see you there!' Dad said, 'Don't be offended Charles. The fact is there is not enough room in the boat for all of us and our gear as well. You take Den and the gear and we will walk up with the dogs.'

They launched the boat at the edge of the river and started to transport the gear from the car and the truck down the bank and stack it next to the boat. Disastrous Den came staggering down the bank with a pack on his back which was the size of your average public telephone box, and if dad hadn't managed to grab him he would have carried on straight into the river and gone down like a deep sea diver. God knows what he had in the pack but when they loaded it the boat sat down four inches lower in the water.

Dad suggested that maybe they should take the gear down in two trips but Captain Charles wouldn't listen and stacked the rest of the gear around and on top of the telephone box shaped backpack. Dad kept the guns on the bank and told them that they would carry them. Grob and I were sitting watching the performance and Grob was grinning. Every time an item went into the boat Grob would say, 'This one should sink it.'

Den climbed on the bow and Charles had left enough space for himself in the stern. The boat was now full and sitting very low in the water. Tony let the other dogs out of Charles's vehicle and they came tearing down the bank. Dad was holding the side of the boat, which was just as well because when Taffy saw Charles in the boat he decided that he would join him and leapt out and landed on top of all the gear. The boat dipped to one side in an attempt to capsize then Taffy fell off it and dad managed to pull the boat upright again before it took in too much water. Lulu started to laugh as Taffy was thrashing around in the water and when Taffy managed to get his paws on the side of the boat and nearly tipped it over again, Grob wet himself.

Taffy eventually managed to climb up the bank from the river and while dad was putting a lead on him he had a good shake and transferred most of the water out of his coat onto dad. Dad shouted, 'Bloody hell Henry! Did you have to do that?' Taffy said, 'They are all the same aren't they? They wait until our coats are full of water and then stand next to us. You would think that after several soakings they might have learnt something. But no, they spend far too long trying to train us when they could do with some training themselves.'

The little engine on the boat started up and it was on its way to the cabin. Dad shouted, 'Bon voyage! We will help you unload when we get there, if you don't sink on the way.'

It was great fun on our way to the cabin. We hunted all the bushes and hedges. Grob and Taffy had quite a few skirmishes trying to determine the pecking order while Lulu and I were busy flushing wild marsh pheasants. Lulu kept talking constantly saying, 'Let's hunt that bush over there Bess, I think there is a pheasant in it. You go round the other side Bess and I will hunt this side. Let's try that hedge over there Bess. Come on Bess, you are going too slow.'

Dad and Tony had a small pack on their backs and were carrying two guns each. They took their time and it took quite a while to walk to the cabin which is nearly three miles

The little boat had done the job and was moored up at the edge of the river adjacent to the cabin and still loaded up with the gear.

Charles and Disastrous Den were standing on the cabin balcony looking out across Pontoon Wash. We walked past them and into the cabin. It looked great with bunk beds, a table with chairs, a sink and a Calor gas oven with cooking rings on the top. There were some good smells in there and I could tell that three other dogs had been in there the day before. I think dad agreed with my theory as he stated that the place stank of bloody dogs.

Dad announced that he was thirsty after the long walk and he suggested that they should unload some of the food and water first and have a cup of tea. This is what they did and when dad passed the bottle of whisky round they all poured a generous measure into their tea. After another pot of tea and an even more generous measure of the dreaded whisky they all seemed extremely happy with life. Tony said, 'You had better unload your barge Charlie, before it gets dark.'

They all went outside and down the steps of the cabin with plenty of giggling going on. Den climbed into the boat and while wobbling about all over the place he started passing the gear out. I was on the bank watching with the other dogs and Lulu was chattering away, 'He's going to fall in. Look at him wobbling I'll bet you he falls in.' There were shouts of, 'I hope you can swim Den because we can't.' from Tony, and they were all being pretty stupid.

It took three of them to pull the telephone box backpack up the bank and the last thing to come out of the boat were dad's hide poles. They were in a long narrow bag and as Disastrous Den passed them up with the bag upside-down a pole slipped out and landed point first between his feet like a javelin. There was another roar of laughter but it was cut short by Charles as he shouted, 'You stupid bastard Den! You have punctured the boat.' Disastrous Den looked down and sure enough the sharp point of the pole was through the hull. He pulled it out and the water started to run in rapidly. He screamed, 'Bloody hell! It's going to sink.' and like a loyal crew member he scrambled up the bank as quickly as he could and abandoned ship. Dad said, 'Somebody get hold of the bow rope with me and help me to pull the boat out.' Well, with much huffing and puffing and a great deal of swearing they dragged the boat, which had taken in a substantial amount of water, up the bank and onto flat ground. Grob and I were in stitches and poor Lulu had lost it completely and was on her back with her legs in the air. Taffy looked about as worried as Charles did, while dad and Tony were trying not to laugh but were not making a very good job of it. Disastrous Den was doing his best to convince everyone that it wasn't his fault while the wart on Charles's nose was changing colour to a luminous pink.

They emptied all the water out of the boat and then stood it up against the cabin steps. There was a hole about half an inch in diameter in the bottom. Tony walked round the other side and started peeping at us through it. Dad couldn't contain himself any longer and burst out laughing while Tony's eye was winking at them. Charles shouted, 'It's not bloody funny you shower of bastards!' Dad said, 'We will have to fix it somehow or we will be walking to The Pickerels tonight.'

Tony came back round from the other side and said, 'The thing to do Charlie is to try and plug the hole.' Charles replied sarcastically, 'What a good idea Tony! Have you got a plug in your pocket?' Tony slowly put his hand in his pocket. Charles immediately said, 'Oh! He is going to plug it with his tobacco tin!' Tony took a penknife out of his pocket and waved it in front of Charles's face and said, 'No, I am not going to waste my tobacco tin on your flimsy boat. I am going to cut that bloody great wart off your nose and stick that in the hole.' Charles's face quickly changed colour to that of the wart like a chameleon would.

Tony rolled a cigarette and lit it before walking over to a bush. He then cut a short stick and walked back. After trying it against the hole he started whittling away at the stick with his knife. In no time at all he had a cone shaped stick that fitted into the hole. He said, 'I need something to seal it.' Dad said, 'I won't be a minute,' and he ran up the cabin steps. He came back with his first aid kit and wrapped the stick with tape. He then pushed the stick into the hole again and with a few taps from the heel of his boot the plug was tight, with just a couple of inches sticking up above the floor of the boat. He then said, 'Let's put it back in the water and see what happens.'

They carried the boat back to the water and lowered it in. The plug held firm apart from a very slow weep. Tony said, 'Bugger me Charlie! We didn't need your wart after all.' Charles stared at Tony and replied. 'Thanks for the repair Tony, but I would appreciate it if you didn't keep referring to my wart.' Tony just smiled and said, 'Okay Charlie,' and then rolled another cigarette.

There were six bunks in the cabin and Den dragged his backpack next to one of them and started to unload it. He had damn near enough stuff in there to furnish the place. Amongst the contents were a camping stove with pots and pans, a fold up chair, a fold up bed with two sleeping bags, a container full of water and four toilet rolls. Dad said, 'Den, I think you have forgotten your washing machine and the tumble dryer.' Den ignored the remark as he carried on taking out his food supply, which was quite substantial. There was a plastic container with half a stone of boiled potatoes, two dozen eggs and half of them were still intact. Tins of beans, salmon and pilchards. Packs of bacon and sausages and packets of soup powder. There were five smaller containers that were all the same size and colour and they all had different things in like salt, pepper, sugar, tea and coffee.

Dad and Tony were grinning to each other as Den carried on emptying and stacking the contents neatly on the bunk. Dad said to Tony, 'Bugger me. He has got a better selection than Tesco's.' Tony grinned and then said, 'We are here for two days Den. Do you think you will have enough food to last out?' Even Charles saw the funny side of that and forced a smile. Den replied, 'I have never been here before so I didn't know what to bring,' as he brought out a pack of six cans of beer. Dad said, 'Essentials at last!' Grob said to me, 'I suppose we could help him out with the food,' and stuck his nose into a pack of sausages. For this kind gesture he received a nudge up the arse from the side of Tony's foot. Grob grinned at me and said, 'See what I mean Bess? I just can't please him.' Den decided to make one of the top bunks his pantry well out of the way of Grob's nose and quickly moved everything up.

Dad suggested that they should try and lighten the return load and offered to fry some of the potatoes Den had brought. They had them with some sausages and eggs and it smelt good. For my dinner I got the spam sandwiches from dad's pocket, which he was going to eat himself before he had seen Den's delicatessen. I hate spam but seeing as there was no choice I had to suffer it.

It was soon time for the trip to The Pickerels for alcohol refreshment. Tony told them that he wasn't bothered about going and offered to stay behind and look after Aladdin's Cave. Charles didn't really want to go either but wouldn't trust dad and Den with his boat, so he reluctantly went with them. Grob wanted to go but wasn't allowed. Taffy told me he detested pubs and wanted to stay behind. So the three men along with Lulu and I set off in the dark heading back up the river the way we had come earlier in the day.

The best way I can describe The Pickerels is likened to a torture chamber for masochists. Dad never stopped complaining about how cold it was in there and how awful the beer was, yet he kept buying more and didn't want to leave. Albert was the name of the landlord and he knew dad from previous trips. When they told him what had happened to the boat he seemed highly amused. One of the locals came in and asked dad if he was wildfowling. Before he had a chance to answer Albert piped up, 'They have been shipwrecked and are waiting to be rescued by the lifeboat.' Charles said, 'I wish someone would rescue us from this freezing hole!' He then stood up and walked out. Dad said to Den, 'I suppose we had better go in a minute,' and then ordered another pint each for them and a couple of bags of crisps for Lulu and me.

When we eventually went outside Charles was sitting in the boat looking pretty miserable. The light from the pub sign was shining on his face exposing his unsightly growth with exaggeration. Dad and Den were in good spirits now and dad said, 'Waarts the matter Charles?' Charles looked at them with contempt as they climbed into the boat while giggling like children.

Everything went well on the way back until we reached the cabin. Dad climbed out first and held the rope. Charles lifted Lulu and me up onto the bank and then climbed out himself. Disastrous Den decided to demonstrate how he had obtained his name. He stood up and as he went to walk forward in the boat he tripped over Tony's plug and hurtled into the freezing water of the Hundred Foot River. I know you shouldn't laugh but Lulu was in hysterics, dad was doubled up and nearly crying and even Charles found it amusing. I must admit I couldn't help but laugh while watching Den scramble back into the boat. Charles helped to pull Den up the bank as he was somewhat heavier now. Dad was in no fit state to help anyone, as he was still doubled up unable to talk.

When we walked into the cabin Tony was reading. He glanced up at Den who was dripping all over the place. Without a smile he said, 'Did you catch anything Den?' 'Only bloody pneumonia.' Den replied.

Tony had lit the oven and the cabin was warm. Den took his wet clothes off and hung them around the oven turning the cabin into a Turkish bath. Tony and dad took chairs out onto the balcony and Grob and I went with them. They sat discussing tactics for morning flight while enjoying a night-cap out of the whisky bottle. Grob said to me, 'It starts to get serious now Bess. Hopefully we will get a few ducks to retrieve in the morning.'

It was a cool night with a new moon trying to make an impression. The clouds were busily racing across the sky and I could hear wigeon and teal calling. The glass of whisky was finished and we all went back inside for some sleep in the sauna. Dad took a bottom bunk and I lay next to him. Grob came over and licked my face and said, 'Goodnight Bess,' as he lay down next to me. Charles selected a bunk as far away from the rest of us as possible and Taffy joined him. They seemed to be a perfect match.

Dad was first up in the morning and put the kettle on the gas ring. There was certainly a sense of excitement about the place. All the bickering and sarcasm seemed to have been forgotten as they put on their waders and shooting gear. Den asked, 'How many cartridges will I need?' Dad replied, 'I always take a full box and a couple of biggies in case the geese come over, but I very rarely use more than ten.'

We went outside and the cabin lights were turned off. It was pitch black as we went down the cabin steps. Dad stopped at the bottom and said, 'Listen to me everyone. We have got plenty of time to get into position so there is no need to rush and have an accident.' Tony added, 'Are you listening Den?' Den replied, 'Yes Tony I am.' Dad then said, 'Just follow me and I will show you where to go.' We slowly walked out onto Pontoon Wash taking a few turns around deep water areas. The wind was stiff but not strong and there was a coldness in the air that makes a dog's nose wet.

After a while dad stopped by a bush and said, 'This can be a good place. Who wants to stand here?' Charles said, 'I will if you want.' Dad replied, 'All right then Charles, but don't shine your torch any more, and don't shoot at the ducks until you can see them properly. When it breaks light keep dead still behind the bush and keep your dog in with you. Only move when you intend to shoot and even then as little as possible.' Charles said, 'So many orders!' Dad replied, 'Listen Charles, and you too Den. Tony and I have been here many times before and too many times the flight has been ruined by people who don't know what they are doing. It is a long way to come so let's try and get it right and shoot as a team and not selfishly. Believe me it will benefit us all.' Charles said. 'All right Vince, point taken.' Dad then said, 'Good luck Charles.' and we walked on and left him and Taffy. Ever since we started this adventure Taffy had looked so miserable. It was easy to tell that he was not impressed with shooting.

A while later we stopped again and Den was put in position. Dad said, 'Good luck Den and no disasters.' Den replied, 'I hope not but I can't offer any guarantees.' As we walked away Lulu said, 'See you later Bess.' I replied, 'Okay Lulu. I hope you get a retrieve.'

We walked on for quite a while without rushing. When we came to a small pond we stopped and Tony tipped some decoys out of his bag. He waded into the water and set the decoys as he wanted them.

Tony then said. 'You stay here Vince, and I will go to the top corner.' He set off with Grob and then it went very quiet.

Dad put his hide poles to the use for what they were intended and built a hide with a small bush as a backdrop. When he was happy with it he took a little folding stool out of his bag and sat on it in the hide. I sat next to him and I was extremely excited. He stroked me and said, 'This is what it is all about young Bess. Sitting out here in the middle of nowhere with you beside me and trying to shoot a duck in their own territory. This is what I love doing and I hope you enjoy it too.' I know he can't hear anything I say so I pushed up tight to his leg and wagged my tail. He recognised my sign and said, 'Good girl, but don't go out for a retrieve until I tell you.'

It seemed to stay dark for a long time and all I could see was an occasional red glow in the distance when Tony took a draw on his cigarette. I started to fidget and dad stroked me again and said, 'You have got to be very patient Bess. Sometimes we will see lots of ducks and other times we won't see any. We have to accept it as it comes.'

As the darkness seemed to be fading into a grey colour some wigeon came over our heads and I could hear their whistling calls clearly. I looked up with surprise but couldn't see anything. Dad put his hand on my back again and said, 'Keep still Bess. Hopefully we will be in business soon.'

The greyness was beginning to lighten and a crow called in the distance. Dad said, 'This is it Bess. Dawn is breaking.' He had no sooner said it than five wigeon flew over the pond out in front of us. He half put his gun up and then took it down again and said, 'Just a bit too far away Bess.' Seconds later I saw a flash from Tony's gun and it was quickly followed by a splash in the water. I looked at dad while waiting for instructions. He said, 'Leave it Bess. Globally will get it later.' I was disappointed but soon forgot about it as a dozen wigeon flew over our heads from behind. Dad threw up his gun and fired both barrels. A bird dropped stone dead to the second shot and landed in the pond thirty yards in front of us. I looked at him again and he said, 'Leave it Bess. It is dead and you can get it later.'

There were quite a few shots going off from the direction where Charles and Den were and then Tony shot another wigeon. A single teal flew across in front and dad dropped it with one shot. The teal hit the water and started splashing about. Dad had a quick look around and then gave me the order I had been waiting for. 'Fetch it Bess.' I didn't need telling twice and I was on my way. As I approached the teal it tried to dive but it wasn't quick enough and I had my first retrieve from the Ouse Washes safely in my mouth. I swam back and gave it to dad and was full of myself. Dad was quick to tell me to sit still and settle down.

It was quite light when a pair of mallard flew over well in range. He missed the pair of them and looked at me as though it was my fault. Tony shot one of them as they flew over him.

There were still a lot of wigeon flying over but it was daylight by now and they were extremely high. We sat there for another hour without a shot being fired and then dad said, 'I think the flight is over. Go and fetch.' I was in the water again and so was Grob. I retrieved the dead duck and was back in time to retrieve one of Grob's that had blown across on the wind. Dad picked up his stool and put it in his bag. Tony soon joined us and Grob said, 'Hey Bess! I saw you taking that duck that should have been mine.' I replied, 'I was just doing what I was told Grob.' He grinned and said. 'I will get my own back. Let's go for a swim now all the fuss is over.'

We both were swimming and it was great. There were trees and bushes on higher ground and we flushed two pheasants out of them. Tony said to dad. 'Look at them two.' Dad replied, 'Let them burn some energy up as they will have nothing to do until this evening.'

Back in the cabin it was time for breakfast and a post-mortem. Tony had shot two wigeon and a mallard. Dad had one wigeon and a teal. Den had one mallard and Charles had nothing except a wart on his nose. Charles said, 'I could have shot at some easy ones but I decided not to be selfish and let them go to Den. The trouble is only one more bunch came my way but they were difficult and I missed them.' Dad said, 'Sometimes it happens like that and sometimes the boot is on the other foot.' Charles responded with, 'I suppose so!'

Dad took on the job of cooking and cooked plenty of sausages and bacon. We all had some and it tasted a lot better than that rotten spam. After we had eaten dad made the tea. He put a small drop of whisky into each pot and handed them round. He then held up his mug and said, 'I would like to propose a toast. To Bess and her first retrieve on the Ouse Washes.' They all said, 'To Bess,' and had a drink. Grob said to me, 'Don't look so coy Bess. It's just another excuse for them to guzzle more whisky.'

After breakfast the men lay on their bunks and it was quiet in the cabin. Grob had taken a fancy to Lulu and was determined to give her one. Lulu had taken evasive action and was lying on the cabin floor with her rear end wedged into a corner to prevent access. Grob was licking her ear telling her how much he liked her when Lulu said,

'Clear off Grob and leave me alone.' Grob replied, 'I only want to talk Lulu.' She then said, 'Bess has told me all about you and I know exactly what you want. And I can tell you now that you are not going to get it so clear off.' It was like water off a duck's back to Grob and he just carried on licking her ear.

Taffy came over and lay down beside me and said, 'Do you really enjoy this fowling Bess?' I replied, 'Yes I love it Taffy. Don't you?' 'No I do not,' he said, 'In actual fact I absolutely hate it.' 'Why is that?' I asked, 'Don't you like retrieving?' Taffy answered, 'I quite like retrieving but the trouble is it never happens. You heard him at breakfast saying that the ducks he missed were difficult. It wouldn't have made any difference if they had been easy, because he would still have missed them. When we lived in Wales he never shot at all but since we left we have been fowling a dozen times or more. In all that time he has taken home just one duck. He told my mum that it was a high fast shot. In actual fact his friend shot it and it landed on the water twenty yards in front of him not quite dead. He fired both barrels at it to finish it off and his friend let him have it.' I said, 'Poor you, did you like it in Wales?' For once Taffy looked relaxed and smiled as he said. 'I lived in the valleys and it was great. Everyone there was friendly and loved to sing. I was a member of the local dogs' choir and I was well respected. Life was wonderful and then he wanted to move and took me away. I think the reason was because he was the only one there that couldn't sing. I love singing and sometimes when I am sitting next to him when we are fowling I get so bored I start to sing. It's a good job they can't hear us talking and singing or we would be in trouble.' He then said, 'It's nice talking to you but I had better go back. He is a loner but he likes me to be near him.' He then stood up and walked over to the far bunk where Charles was lying.

At three in the afternoon Den spotted some geese and all the men started to get excited. They put their gear on and we were off early for the evening flight. The geese disappeared into the distance and were not seen again. We sat there until it was pitch black, and regardless of dad telling me about ten times that the flight should start in a minute, we only saw two ducks and nobody fired a shot.

That night they decided to stay in the cabin and finish off the cans of beer and what was left of the whisky. It's amazing how they change when alcohol gets into their bodies. They were all telling stories and when Charles told them how he regularly shoots ten ducks on his fowling trips, Taffy looked at me and smiled as he muttered, 'Bloody liar!'

When the booze had ran out they climbed into their bunks. I must admit I liked it in the cabin. It was certainly different from everyday life and there was always that feeling that the next flight was going to be a good one. Lulu had decided it would be safer to sleep in the corner of the cabin and Grob slept with one eye open in case she moved. I lay next to dad and fell asleep.

We were up early again and the excitement in the cabin was mounting. Dad walked out onto the balcony and came back in saying that the weather conditions were perfect, and maybe those geese will come back and fly over us. Den and Charles had been talking and had decided to switch positions for this flight, so now Taffy would be closer to me.

Lights out and down the cabin steps for our last flight. The wind had picked up and was blowing quite strong. We slowly walked across the wash to our positions. As we left Charles I said, 'Good luck Taffy,' He replied, 'You must be joking Bess. He's got more chance of being struck by lightning than hitting a duck.'

Dad adjusted the hide and Tony rearranged the decoys. We sat and waited for the light to break and dad was stroking me. He said, 'I have a feeling that this is going to be a good flight Bess.' I wagged my tail and thought to myself, that's what he thought last night too.

As the light started to break about ten wigeon flew across the pond in front of us. Dad only had time to fire one barrel but managed to hit one of them and it plummeted into the water. Just a couple of seconds after dad's shot Tony took one out as well. There were two ducks down so Grob and I were going to get at least one each to retrieve.

Daylight came very quickly and the wigeon were flighting well. The problem was they seemed to have a definite flight line and that was straight over the top of Charles. Every five minutes or so a bunch would fly over him at about thirty yards and Charles would blast away with two barrels, but not a feather came down. The wigeon just kept on coming until nine o'clock but nobody else got a shot at them. Every single bunch took the safe route over Charles.

He had fired just about a box full of cartridges when I heard something that I will never forget for as long as I live. A beautiful unaccompanied tenor voice started singing, 'We'll keep a welcome in the hillside. We'll keep a welcome in the dales.' Taffy had given up on Charles and was doing what he enjoyed most.

The wigeon were still flighting but were now at a much higher altitude so Grob and I were sent out to retrieve the two ducks. As I was swimming back I looked across and Taffy was watching me. I felt really sorry for him. Dad packed up the hide and we all headed back to the cabin.

There was a weird atmosphere in the cabin while dad was cooking breakfast. Everyone knew that Charles should have had a bag full but didn't like to say anything. Tony broke the ice with, 'I reckon that they must have seen your wart Charlie and then climbed in height out of range.' Charles looked daggers at Tony and said, 'It's the cartridges. I tried a different make and they are bloody useless.' Taffy grinned and said to me, 'Not as bloody useless as him though!'

Den took the plate that had his breakfast on over to the bunk which was acting as his pantry. He reached up and put his fingers into the little pot which he thought contained the salt. Unfortunately, he sprinkled his breakfast with sugar. That was a bit of luck for us dogs because once dad had washed the sugar off, it didn't taste too bad at all.

They started to pack the gear in the boat for our trip home. There was nowhere near as much weight in the boat as there had been when we came because the greedy sods had eaten and drunk most of it, but there was still plenty of bulk. Dad and Tony walked again and we hunted the bushes on the way back.

When we arrived home mum was pleased to see us. While dad unloaded the truck mum gave me a bath. She said, 'I have saved you something special for your dinner Bess.' She dried me off with a towel and I was hungry and couldn't wait to see my special treat. Mum took it out of the fridge and as she put it in my dish she said, 'There you are Bess. You enjoy it.' It was the rest of the tin of that bloody spam.

Dad came up the stairs and had a shower while mum cooked their dinner. They had a piece of steak each with all the trimmings. I was sitting watching them as they cut the brown crispy fat off the edge of their steaks and left it on their plates. I thought that I was going to get it but dad said to mum, 'Put that fat in the bin. I don't want the dog to put any weight on.' I thought, wonderful! He doesn't worry too much about weight when he is swilling pints of beer and guzzling whisky.

Mum put the fat in a bag and then put it in the pedal bin in the kitchen before she started washing up. Dad said, 'Come on Bess. Let's go and sit by the fire.' We went into the sitting room and he sat in his chair. I sat at his feet and watched him as he started to nod. I crept out and back into the kitchen where mum was. I then sat by the pedal bin and put on my best 'Poor me' looking face. Mum glanced in the sitting room and saw him sleeping. She came back and took the fat out of the bin and gave it to me. I wagged my tail in delight and licked my lips for five minutes afterwards.

We both went back in the sitting room and mum sat in her chair. I took up my rightful place on the rug in front of the fire and thought about our adventure. I wondered where Taffy would be. I then thought, probably listening to Charles telling a pack of lies somewhere. Shame about Charles's boat, although it did provide a good laugh. I couldn't help smiling as I thought of the serene sound of, 'We'll keep a welcome in the hillside. We'll keep a welcome in the dales.' Drifting across the wildness of the Ouse Washes.

CHAPTER 6

Beating and the Christmas party

We were on the road again for another session of beating. Dad was looking forward to it because when this day's beating was finished there was to be a Christmas party. Mum was with us and was going to go back with the vehicle. She would then collect us later that evening when dad was full up with whisky. I had been to this place before but I was not impressed.

We turned off the main road and followed narrow country lanes as we drove towards the massive house. It looked more like a castle with lawns and ponds in front of it. We drove past the house and into a yard where there were a lot of stables that were in desperate need of repair. The doors were hanging off some of them and on others the roofs had collapsed. At the end of the stable block was an old house, which was in a similar state as the stables but maybe not quite as bad. There was a group of people gathered outside the door and a lot of dogs milling around. The biggest selection of misfits you could ever put together and it is incredible where they all come from. A film director would have to spend many years auditioning before he could have come up with a cast like this lot.

I recognised most of them from before and I was surprised that some of them were still alive. Amongst the more normal ones there was a man with a potbelly called Wally. He was talking to a man that was permanently bent over called Stoop. Poor Stoop had a rather large hump that looked like a backpack under his coat. There was Ernie who is one of those people who has not only done everything that is mentioned, but he has also done it better than anyone else. Then there was Ned. He waves a bag at the edge of the woods to stop the birds breaking out. Ned has a stick that a pole-vaulter would be proud of and has a bag permanently tied to it. He insists on taking it into the beater's wagon with him and over the course of the day he will have caused grief and suffering to everyone else at some stage or other. There was a scruffy looking weasel type man with massive dark bags under his eyes who never stops popping pills into his mouth. They call him Flash and after nearly every statement he makes he says, 'Am I right then. Am I right?' He was talking to Mick, who is in the same syndicate as dad. Over the other side of the group were three of the laziest specimens you will ever see. Youths about eighteen years old who were on the dole and have never done a day's work in their lives. Their camouflage gear were the replica football shirts from the two major Glasgow teams. Two were blue Rangers colours and the other one in the green and white hoops of Celtic. They always stuck together and had been given the names, Can't, Won't and Willnot. Behind them were Bonnie and Clyde. They are a young couple who can't keep their hands off each other and will spend most of the day locked in passionate embraces.

There was a mixed bunch of dogs as well, which included a couple of flatcoats called Susie and Sal. They were always talking about other dogs and were the biggest gossips I have ever met. What they didn't know about the other dogs they made up as they went along. There was a very aggressive Jack Russell called Jack who was always looking for a scrap. An Irish water spaniel called Paddy who belonged to Mick. Paddy's language was somewhat educational to a young shy dog like myself. There was a collie with a limp we called Hoppy, a cocker spaniel who was deaf called Bonzo and a Labrador called Rita who was pregnant.

While I was looking and thinking that my dad was fairly normal compared to this lot Tony and Grob arrived. The first thing that Grob said was, 'Where's Silver?' He was referring to the keeper who was going to try and take control of the proceedings. Some years ago he had been involved in an accident and now has an artificial leg and a glass eye. The leg worked well but the glass eye looked like a large marble so he always wore an eye patch to cover it. The only thing missing was the parrot and that is why he was called Silver. He lived in the broken down house where the Christmas party was going to be held. I said to Grob, 'He hasn't come out yet but when he does I'll bet Jack has a go at his dog.' Sure enough five minutes later out he came with his black Labrador called Teal, walking to heel in a perfect manner. As they walked past the bunch of dogs an evil looking black and white bundle of muscles took his chance and Jack leapt out and grabbed a mouthful of Teal's ear. All hell let loose for a few minutes with horrendous squeals from Teal and it took three belts with the stick and a kick in the goolies before Jack would let go. Paddy said to Bonzo, 'That Jack is a fecking eejit. He always picks on a dog three times his size. Bonzo being deaf said, 'Aye.' Paddy repeated himself but louder and once again Bonzo said, 'Aye.' Paddy looked at him and said, 'Feck off you deaf bastard,' then Bonzo who still hadn't heard a word said, 'Yes, but I think it's going to rain later.'

The under-keeper who was called Spud came out next. He had a shaved head apart from a narrow strip of hair down the centre, which was dyed purple. I remembered him from before, only the strip of hair had changed colour from red, and he looked more suited to be in a rock band than on a shoot. He was the clumsiest person you would ever see and spent more time horizontal on the ground than he did standing.

There was a tractor, which had a makeshift trailer behind it. The trailer looked as though it had been put together with some of the stable doors that were hanging off and the roof on it was old corrugated tin sheets that were blowing about and rattling. One of them looked as though it was about to part company with the others at any minute. If the Health and Safety at Work Officer had seen the contraption they would have locked Silver up and thrown the key away.

Silver gave the order and we all piled into the trailer. Wally was the first victim of the pole-vaulter's weapon as it was thrust into his potbelly. Wally screamed out in agony, and as he lifted his jumper up to examine the damage another button gave up trying to contain the bulge and pinged off his shirt. Someone at the other end of the trailer shouted, 'Put it away Wally.' He rubbed the floppy mass that was hanging over his trousers and then covered it up again. Ned was on the other end of the pole but was totally oblivious to what had happened.

Bonnie and Clyde had found a corner at the top end of the trailer and he was now trying to lose his tongue down her throat. As the trailer lurched forward I think she would have swallowed his false teeth as well if he had any. Flash took a little bottle out of his pocket and tipped two pills into the palm of his hand. Transferring them to his mouth he gulped them down. This was followed by some vigorous shaking of the head and two minutes later he was a different person while laughing and smiling at absolutely nothing at all.

Rita was sitting next to me and I said to her, 'When is the happy event?' She replied, 'I have still got five weeks to go but I can feel them kicking sometimes.' Sal piped up, 'Who is the father this time Rita?' She replied, 'Wouldn't you like to know.' Susie joined in now with, 'I bet you would like to know as well Rita,' and both the flatcoats burst out laughing. When they stopped laughing Grob said with a grin on his face, 'I wish it was me.' Susie said, 'If it isn't you

Grob it wouldn't be from the lack of trying,' and Susie and Sal were laughing again.

The trailer stopped in a field and we were ordered to get out just in time for three Range Rovers to drive up alongside and try and run over me and the rest of the dogs. There was a scramble as the owners tried to rescue their dogs and that resulted in Spud's first encounter of the day with the ground. I don't know how it happened because I was trying to avoid a Goodyear tread at the time, although I think Ned's stick could well have had something to do with it, but whatever it was Spud was lying flat in the mud, belly side down.

The occupants of the vehicles were the guns and what a beefy lot they were. The hip flasks were being drained already and they hadn't even fired a shot. The man in charge, who is the owner of the estate and was dressed like a clown, got out of the front vehicle and started issuing the orders. Silver immediately went into his Uriah Heep routine and was bowing and scraping and screwing his cap up in his hands. 'Yes ma-lord, no ma-lord, three bags full ma-lord, kiss your arse ma-lord.'

The clown climbed back in the vehicle and they sped off spraying the beaters with mud from their wheels. Flash said, 'What a shower of bastards! Am I right then? Am I right?' Silver replied, 'You are right Flash but don't upset them because I am hoping for some decent Christmas tips.'

The first drive was a narrow wood that had a fast flowing stream down one side. The ground dropped away from it into a valley and that is where the guns were to stand. The beaters split into two parties and came in from each end of the wood. Ned stayed outside the wood near the centre on the opposite side from the stream to wave his bag and discourage the pheasants from flying out that way.

We slowly worked the birds to the centre of the wood and they started to break out and fly over the guns with the strong wind behind them. We were way above the guns and some of them were shooting at the birds while they were well out in front. Suddenly, Flash yelled out in pain as he dropped onto his knees while holding his ear. He shouted, 'The bastards have shot me!' And a trickle of blood started to run down his face. Silver ran to the edge of the stream and shouted down to the guns, 'Don't shoot the bloody beaters!' And then remembering his potential Christmas tips quickly added, 'Sir,' but the guns carried on blasting regardless. Dad and I were working the strip at the side of the stream and dad put his hood up for protection.

The last dozen or so pheasants took to the air and one of the guns took one very early. The bird was hit but it turned and glided back towards the wood crashing into the stream fifty yards in front of us. Rita was at the side of the stream and jumped straight in for a retrieve. The stream was really flowing and Rita was now heading down towards us at a rate of knots and totally out of control. Dad dropped onto his knees at the edge of the stream and as Rita was being washed past us he grabbed her tail. She squealed but he didn't let go until he had pulled her out. I think dad saved her life, not to mention the future family.

That was the drive over and we made our way back. Flash had a pellet in the lobe of his ear and it is amazing how so much blood could come out of such a little hole. We climbed back into the trailer and Flash was shaking. He took out his bottle and tipped three pills into his palm. He was shaking so much they fell on the floor and Jack pounced and swallowed them in a split second. Flash gave up the idea of tipping them into his palm and tipped the next lot straight into his mouth. Another ten seconds of head shaking and he calmed down and started to smile again.

Unfortunately, the pills had the opposite effect on Jack and he became extremely violent and started to bite everything within range, which included men and dogs. Jack emptied the trailer in fifteen seconds flat and was creating havoc. Paddy said, 'The fecking eejit has gone berserk!' And then dived under the trailer. I followed him while Jack was running amok and his dad was running after him trying to put a lead on him.

After tearing around for two minutes and sinking his teeth into everything in sight he flopped down onto the ground and passed out. His dad picked him up and carried him back into the trailer and we all climbed in again. Jack's eyes were rolling but he seemed to have a smile on his face. Jack's dad said to Flash, 'What the hell is in those pills?' He replied, 'I don't really know but they cheer me up,' and then smiled and said, 'Am I right then. Am I right?'

The trailer was now on the move to the next drive. After about five minutes Jack started to come round. His dad had a lead on him, not knowing what to expect. Jack opened his eyes and said, 'Where am I? What happened?' Paddy answered, 'There is one thing for certain Jack, you won't pass a fecking drugs test at the end of the day!'

We came to a bumpy halt as the driver of the tractor decided to put the beaters through an endurance test and parked it in the middle of a disused quarry. Clyde reluctantly released himself from the clinch he was in with Bonnie and they both surfaced for air. Bonnie's makeup was evenly distributed between their two faces.

Silver ordered us all out of the trailer and the Range Rovers, which were more like mobile distilleries, once more tried to exterminate the team. The guns were really getting into the swing of things now and they were certainly more lively, or pissed, than they had been when we last saw them. The windows of the vehicles were open and it looked more like a smokehouse in there with half of the occupants hanging on the end of a King Edward cigar and the other half polishing off gin and whisky through the neck of the bottles. Behind the Range Rovers were two older and cheaper versions of four-wheel drive vehicles and these were the picking-up brigade.

A man in the passenger seat of the front picking-up vehicle, whose name was Lionel, looked out of the window at us and started to grin. I was beginning to feel rather embarrassed to be part of the beating team. Stoop who had been pretty quiet up to now was grumbling about how Jack had given him a rough time when he was away with the fairies, and how he had chased him all over the place and had worn him out. He was bent over even more than usual and if his neck had been a little longer you could have easily mistaken him for a camel. Ned was going through a practice routine, waving his bag in the air on the end of his flagpole as though he was about to lead an army into battle. The more pills Flash devoured the darker the patches under his eyes were becoming and he was starting to look more like a panda. Clyde had now pinned Bonnie up against the trailer and you wouldn't have squeezed a cigarette paper between them. Can't, Won't and Willnot were in a huddle arguing about football and looked as though they might have been waiting for a match to start. Ernie was telling Spud and Tony about how he had just come back from a shoot where he was a loader for Prince Charles and Tony was looking at him as much as to say, 'Bloody liar!' Potbelly had found a deep hole and was sitting on the ground with his legs dangling in it. The keeper looked like a bloody pirate and the under-keeper like a punk rocker.

Susie and Sal had noticed a chocolate Labrador bitch in the back of the picking-up vehicle and they were giving her a good slagging off. Sal said, 'I heard that she was serviced four times in one day by different dogs.' Susie replied, 'No wonder she has got a smile on her face,' and they went into another hysterical huddle. Jack had spotted a German pointer in the same vehicle and was in the process of trying to tear the back door off its hinges in his desperation to get at it for a fight. Hoppy was running around in circles on three legs and Grob was trying to talk to Bonzo. Grob said, 'How are you Bonzo?' He replied, 'About twelve o'clock I think.'

The clown half fell out of the vehicle and he had quite a glow on. He said to Silver, 'I want the beaters to put more effort into this drive and don't go so bloody fast.' Silver grovelled and said, 'Do you realise that the guns shot one of the beaters on the last drive ma-lord?' The clown looked at the bunch of misfits and replied, 'Never mind. There are plenty of you.' This brought a great roar of laughter from the occupants of the Range Rovers and one them, who was in the process of draining another gin bottle when he heard the remark, started choking. I heard Flash mutter, 'Die you rich bastard, die!'

The vehicles sped off again and Silver, with some help from Spud, managed to get his gang to pay attention and we all walked across a field at the back of the quarry. We came to a wood, which was shaped like a wedge, and about five hundred yards long. It was quite wide at the end where we started to drive it, but it narrowed in to a point at the other end. The guns were at the bottom, set out in the shape of a horseshoe, with some of the guns up each side of the wood. The picking-up brigade were poised behind them.

Dad and I were positioned on the outside and it was easy walking. Silver gave the instructions to start and the noise of screeching and shouting from some of the beaters started to ring out through the wood. I don't know why beaters make so much noise because it is more likely to frighten the pheasants and make them sit tight. I think they do it to give themselves a sore throat so they can ease the pain with ten pints of beer afterwards.

We slowly worked forward and pheasants were breaking out constantly. I had some gorse bushes to work and some of them had five or six birds sitting tight underneath them. The guns were being kept busy and amongst them there were some pretty good shots. It was great fun flushing the birds out and being able to see them flying over the guns. When you are in the middle of the wood you never see that.

We were now approaching the end of the drive and the point of the wood. Each step forward brought us closer together as the wood narrowed. There was a clump of bracken at the end and it was loaded with pheasants. Some of the dogs were working it and the birds were rising in bunches. The guns shouldn't complain about that drive, they must have had five hundred birds over them.

All of a sudden a black and white tornado went speeding past me totally flat out. Jack had spotted the German pointer going for a retrieve and was heading for him with flames coming out of his arse. Paddy, who was now next to me said, 'Jeezus! Look at the size of that pointer he is about to attack. I told you he was a fecking eejit.' Jack's dad was screaming at him but Jack had shut his ears and the only thing on his mind was blood. I don't think he really cared whether it was his own or the pointers, but blood it was going to be.

The pointer had just picked the pheasant up when Jack hit him with a broadside. This resulted in both dogs rolling for about ten yards and a great bunch of feathers flying into the air. They picked themselves up and Jack went in for another charge. As he approached, the pointer did a clever side step and grabbed Jack by the back of the neck. He then lifted him off the ground and started to shake him vigorously. Jack looked like a rag doll and didn't have a chance while his feet were off the ground. After about a minute Jack's dad arrived on the scene and with the help of three other men they managed to get the dogs apart. Jack was brought back on a lead and looked a bit groggy to say the least. Paddy said to him, 'Is it fecking stupid that you are Jack? That German is five times bigger than you.' Jack shook himself and replied, 'The Kraut was lucky that time, but I will have the bastard before the day is over.'

That was the fun over for the morning and we went back for lunch. The stately dining hall for us was one of the broken down stables that must have had six horses in it at some time. There was a large table in the centre with seat benches each side of it. There was also a smaller table at the side of the wall that had a stack of dishes on a little stool next to it. They looked as though they could have done with a wash and two spiders were having a fight over a fly in the top dish.

The whole place was absolutely filthy. Silver announced, 'Molly will be in with the soup in a minute,' and then he pushed the stable door open wide. I soon realised why, as an extremely stout lady came in carrying a large pan of soup while singing a song from The Sound of Music. She was in her middle forties and about twenty stone. Her face was round and plump and her body had a roly-poly shape. No doubt you have seen the Michelin man, well here was Michelin woman. On her head was a bonnet that would have been more suitable for an Easter parade or a day at Ascot. It had six large brightly coloured flowers evenly placed all the way around it, except for one which was hanging off.

As she shuffled over to the table she sang, The hills are alive with the sound of music, and then dumped the pan down on the table with such force that some of the contents spilled over the side and onto the filthy table. She took a dirty cloth out of her pocket and with the other hand lifted the top dish where the fight was still going on. She then used the cloth to push the spilt soup into the dish and duly tipped it back into the pan again, spiders, fly, dirt and all.

The brown rat that had been hiding under the stool decided that it was far too dirty in there for it and made a dash for the open door. It only made halfway as Jack was on it like a flash and killed it instantly with one shake. Dad said jokingly, 'Well at least we will now have some meat for the party tonight Molly.' She replied quite seriously, 'It wouldn't be the first time we have eaten rat.'

Molly served up the soup which was virtually clear. Dad took a spoonful and said, 'Is it water flavoured soup Molly?' She replied, 'Don't blame me. His Lordship said I was spending too much on the beaters' soup and I had to cut the powder down by half.' Dad left his but Won't, Can't and Willnot had two bowls full each with as much bread as they could scrounge from the other beaters, which was a bit of a nuisance because I could have done without the competition.

Bonnie and Clyde were in an embrace at the end of the table and Clyde looked as though he was trying to empty the wax contents out of Bonnie's right ear with his tongue. All the time the beaters were eating Molly was going through her selection of songs from musicals. I suppose it would have been nice if she could sing, or even had sung in tune, but her voice was so shrill that it made me and all the others shudder.

Molly collected in the bowls from the table. She then took out her cloth and rubbed it over the tabletop stopping half way to blow her nose on the cloth. That was the cleaning done and she made a musical exit with the pan and the remaining liquid.

Five minutes later she returned with a cash box and a book. She started to pay the beaters and each time she paid one she placed the book in front of them and said, 'Sign for it!' She worked her way around the table and Clyde took the opportunity of the interruption to change ears. Dad was paid last just after Won't, Can't and Willnot. When we walked outside dad said to Tony, 'I didn't realise we were in such important company.' Tony replied, 'There is nobody important amongst that lot.' Dad said, 'Well, the three signatures before mine were, Winston Churchill, Wyatt Earp and Mickey Mouse.' Tony replied, 'That's them idle bastards in the football shirts who are on the dole. They are frightened that the DSS finds out that they come here.'

We climbed into the trailer again and Ned threw his lance in. Wally with the potbelly saw it coming and picked Paddy up, using him as a shield. The deadly stick went straight into the rear end of Paddy and he shrieked, 'Jeezus, Mary and Joseph. Is it a fecking kebab yous are trying to make me into?'

The tractor set off down the track for the afternoon session. Bonnie had now latched on to the side of Clyde's neck and was sucking like a vampire, while Clyde was trying to clear the excess ear wax out from between his teeth. Flash threw an empty pill bottle out of the back of the trailer and took out another full one from his pocket. Hoppy forgot about his bad leg and leapt out of the back of the trailer to retrieve the bottle, landing in a great heap in the middle of the track. Paddy said, ' Jeezus! He must have been on the pills as well, he thinks he can fecking well fly.' Sal said to Susie, 'I don't think I can take much more of this,' and burst into laughter. Susie had tears running down her face as they went into another huddle. Dad pushed Ned's stick through a hole in front of the trailer and banged on the rear of the tractor with it. The tractor stopped and Hoppy was scraped up off the track and dumped back in the trailer.

When the tractor stopped again the mobile distilleries were already there, and what a good lunch the occupants must have had. Mainly liquid by the state of them, because their faces were glowing and they all had permanent stupid grins. We climbed out and Flash immediately said to Wally, 'Oh no! We are going to do the Plantation Bog.'

The clown was too pissed to get out of the vehicle so he summoned Silver over to him, and with a definite slur he said to him, 'I want all the beaters to work properly this time. There may be a lot of woodcock in there and I want them all flushed out.' Silver replied sheepishly, 'Well ma-lord, we had a lot of rain last week and there will be a lot of water in there, maybe three feet deep in places.' The clown replied, 'Don't worry about getting wet man, just do it properly.' Silver started to screw his cap up again and replied, 'Yes ma-lord, of course ma-lord.'

The Range Rovers set off again and I could hear the occupants laughing as they went. Spud said to dad, 'I hate this drive, it is so slippery.' Paddy said to me, 'He can't even stay upright on dry ground, he will have no chance in there!' I had never been to this drive before so I asked, 'Is it bad Paddy?' He replied, 'It is awful for them, but not too bad for us because we have four legs.'

We walked across several fields until we came to the top of a hill. It was quite a climb and even Bonnie and Clyde had to separate their mouths for a minute to do some deep breathing. Wally was puffing and blowing and Stoop's nose was nearly touching the ground. Flash looked totally knackered but soon recharged his battery with another intake of pills.

There was a large valley below us with a narrow plantation situated along it. I could see some of the guns staggering down the hill to their pegs, which were set all around the plantation. Flash said to Wally, 'This is a useless pheasant drive as they come out too low, but these rich bastards just love to have a shot at the woodcock, so keep your head down.'

We walked down to the valley and lined out along the edge of the wood. Silver gave the signal and we started to walk. It soon became very wet and many of the trees had blown over but were still alive, creating large obstacles which the beaters had to climb over. I looked across just in time to see Spud lose his balance while on top of one of the fallen trees. He went into a pike dive with a twist and two backward somersaults and entered the water with a splash, which would have lost him points had there been judges.

We were going through a mixture of either deep water or bog and it looked to me as though nothing would want to live in there, but within minutes of us starting, woodcock, snipe and pheasants were on the move. The guns were blasting away again and you could sometimes hear the pellets hitting the trees. I don't know what prize they get for a right and a left at beaters, but they seemed hell bent on getting one. Stoop found it easier than most of the others because he was permanently bent over, but now all the others were walking as if they were mimicking him. I heard Silver shouting at Bonnie and Clyde to keep their heads down and I looked across. Clyde had picked up Bonnie and was carrying her through two feet of water, while she was conscientiously working on another giant love bite on his neck to match the one she had industriously created on the opposite side. They totally ignored Silver and just carried on in their own little world with pellets flying around them.

We slowly worked our way through and the beaters were struggling. Each time I looked at Spud he was either trying to get up or in the process of falling down. More by luck than judgement we managed to reach the end of the plantation without any losses. The beaters gathered into a huddle and the steam was rising from them.

The clown had managed to stagger down the hill to his peg with the help of one of the picking-up brigade but he was too pissed and too heavy to walk back up the hill again. After desperately trying to assist him, and making no progress whatsoever, the man was instructed to go and bring the Range Rover. This he duly did and the clown was helped into the front passenger seat. When the vehicle tried to climb the hill again it started to sink in the wet ground and after some severe revving of the engine and spinning of the wheels it was nearly down to the axles. The nicely dressed picking-up brigade were now ordered to give the vehicle a push. They reluctantly followed orders but didn't managed to move it an inch, although they did collect a barrow full of mud from the vehicle's wheels, which was plastered all the way up their fronts. The clown ordered another Range Rover to pull that one out. Down the hill it came and a rope was tied between them. The driver revved the engine and the vehicle sank without tightening the rope.

The guns had now congregated around the vehicles and had decided to lighten the load by drinking more gin. Sal said, 'Come on boys, bring the other Range Rover down and you can go for a hat trick.' Paddy said, 'I thought it was the Irish that are supposed to be thick.' Susie said, 'You suppose bloody right Paddy,' and the pair of them were laughing again. Paddy then said quite seriously, 'Listen yous bastards. Don't think I'm not an eejit,' and he couldn't understand why the rest of us dogs then started laughing as well.

The beaters were now ordered to go over and they tried to help by pushing but it was a hopeless cause. The remaining Range Rover was sent to tell the tractor driver to come and rescue them. The tractor came down the hill with the trailer attached and with a great struggle the guns were loaded into it and then transported back to the road. It is incredible that the guns had no qualms about sending the beaters through Plantation Bog and yet they were not even capable of walking up the hill themselves. The tractor then unhooked from the trailer and came back and pulled out one of the Range Rovers towing it back to the road. It was while it was on its way back that the action started again.

The German pointer and Jack had been glaring at each other for quite a while. Jack was on his starting blocks just raring to go. Paddy said, 'Be wise Jack. You will only get another fecking hiding.' Jack replied, 'Don't you be so sure Paddy. I will have that Kraut yet.' Paddy said, 'What the hell have you got against the Germans anyway?' Jack replied, 'The bastards bombed my great, great, great grandfather's kennel and flattened it.'

The pointer turned to watch the tractor returning and Jack took his chance. He sped over and latched his powerful jaws around the back leg of the pointer, and no matter how the pointer tried he couldn't get at Jack. As he turned one way Jack shuffled across the other way and as the pointer went the other way Jack shuffled back again. The pointer was obviously in severe pain and was making some terrible noises. Soon there were four men trying to part them and they had to force Jack's mouth open to release his victim. They were both put on leads and the pointer was limping very badly. Jack had a grin on his face that would last for a long time. He was brought back and said, 'That's one for my ancestors.'

The pointer belonged to Lionel and he was not at all pleased. He shouted, 'You bloody beaters don't know how to train a dog, they are all bloody wild.' Wally replied, 'At least our dogs work. Yours are just a load of wankers!' Lionel passed the dog lead to his colleague and then walked across and stood in front of Wally. He glared at him and said, 'Would you like to repeat that.' Wally replied, 'Why, are you bloody deaf or something?' Lionel was really angry now and said, 'I have a good mind to teach you a lesson.' Wally replied, 'Would that be a lesson on how to lick the boots of the guns and creep up their arses?' The tractor arrived just in time and Lionel had to go and help with the rope. As he walked away he said, 'I will sort you out later Wally.' 'I will look forward to it,' replied Wally. 'See you at the party.'

So much time had been taken with the rescue it was decided to cancel the last drive. It was just as well because most of the guns were just about legless. We climbed into the trailer and were heading back to the stables. The trailer had a strong smell of alcohol which the guns had left behind.

Flash was looking rather uncomfortable and was holding his stomach. He suddenly stood up, bent right over and then let rip with a tremendous fart out of the rear end. Just as he did it, a gust of wind blew underneath the loose corrugated roof sheet and it finally conceded defeat and went spinning through the air. Paddy immediately said, 'Jeezus Mary and Joseph! Now that is what I call a proper fecking fart. He has blown the fecking roof off.'

We arrived back and everyone climbed out of the trailer and stood in a group. After a few minutes a car was driven into the yard and a man wearing a suit and carrying a briefcase got out and walked towards the house. Wally said, 'I wonder who that is?' Tony replied, 'I have seen him before. He is from the DSS.' Well, panic set in and I have never seen such a scramble as the bunch of beaters were suddenly reduced to just four. There were bodies darting into every conceivable hiding place. Tony then said to dad, 'I was telling porky pies. I know him well and he is really the game feed representative, but I will let them sweat a bit longer. I am going in to have a chat with him.' After a while the man came out of the house and drove off. Tony followed him out as the bodies started to crawl from out of the woodwork looking quite frightened. Tony shouted, 'He is looking for Winston Churchill and Mickey Mouse.' One of the lazy youths said, 'He didn't mention Wyatt Earp, did he?'

Dad took his beating gear off and gave me a good rub with a towel. He said to me, 'You are not very clean Bess but you are cleaner than the house will be.' Everyone had been instructed to bring something to drink and Silver and Molly were providing the food. Dad took a bottle of whisky out of the car and he then took me into the house.

Dad was right, it was absolutely filthy. There must have been nearly an inch of mud on the floor. We went through into quite a large room and there was a table with glasses on it. There were some bottles of gin and vodka on there and dad put his bottle of whisky with them and then sat in a chair. I sat next to him and gazed around the room. There were heaps of sandwiches on plates placed on dressers and sideboards which were against the walls with some paper plates in a pile. Tony came and sat next to dad and Grob sat next to me. Grob had been very quiet today and had kept out of trouble for once.

The rest of the beaters started to come in and put on the table what they had brought to drink. Most of them had a bottle of something or other, but the three lazy football supporters brought two cans of lager between them.

Bonnie and Clyde came in and what a transformation. She had taken all the waterproof gear off and was dressed to kill. She had a short skirt on which was more like a pelmet and the low cut tight fitting top she was wearing was struggling to keep everything in. She sat on a settee and crossed her legs showing everyone opposite her knickers. All the men were staring lustfully at her and Clyde did what he had been doing all day. He just lay on top of her spoiling the view.

All of the beaters were in but we were waiting for the picking-up lot to arrive before getting stuck into the food. Ten minutes later they did arrive, wearing their fancy jumpers with their whistles still around their necks. Jack was disappointed as Lionel walked in because he had wisely left the pointer in his vehicle. They had brought some wine and started to speak to each other in rather posh voices.

A few moments later there was the awful shrill of Molly's voice as she entered the room singing, Onward Christian Soldiers, and carrying the soup that had been left over from the lunch-time session. She had really dressed for the occasion and put on a long dress, which had hundreds of worn threads dragging on the hard baked mud floor. Her cheeks had been enhanced with two large dollops of dark orange rouge and she had enough bright red lipstick spread around her mouth to last any normal woman a month or two. The over the top mascara was on thick and looked as though it could have been applied with the back of a shovel. She still had on her favourite hat but the loose flower had fallen off somewhere and there was now just a space where it had been hanging.

Molly screeched, 'There you are my friends, get stuck in!' The three yobs moved far quicker than they had done all day and acquired a bowl of soup each, absconding into a corner with a plate full of sandwiches. Spud joined them and the rest of the crew took a paper plate each and started a sort of examination of the rest of the sandwiches. They were massive bread wedges, which looked as though they had been roughly cut with a chainsaw. The men were walking around the room in an organised line going from plate to plate, picking up a sandwich and then quickly putting it down again, until they arrived back at where they had started without actually having been brave enough to take one. Clyde wasn't in the mood for food as he still had his nose buried deep into Bonnie's cleavage, while she was stroking the back of his head and moaning.

Molly picked up a plate of the sandwiches and said, 'Come on you lot, eat up. I did these fresh for you the day before yesterday.' She then started to distribute a couple onto everybody's plate, whether they wanted them or not.

Dad picked one up and opened it carefully as though it was going to explode. He examined the contents and said, 'Bess, you can have this,' and took out the filling and passed it down to me. It was a small piece of ham which was so thinly cut I could see dad's leg through it. I ate it anyway and Grob was quite happy to swallow the chunks of bread. One gulp and they were gone and I could actually see the lump sticking out of the skin of his neck as it went down. Another thin slice of ham for me and another half a loaf for Grob and the eating formalities were over.

Most of the sandwiches had been pushed down the side of the chairs or underneath, and Grob spent the rest of the evening trying to get them out. Molly collected in the plates and then the drinking started.

First at the drinks table were the football boys and Spud. They discarded the two cans of lager and poured four rather large glasses from dad's whisky bottle and then went back into a huddle in the corner. I looked at dad and could see he was angry because his eye started twitching. When it came to his turn three-quarters of his bottle had gone. He poured one for himself and sat down again muttering to Tony, 'If they all like whisky so much why didn't they bloody well bring some?' Ernie, the compulsive liar, was bending Silver's ear with his unbelievable stories because nobody else would listen.

It is amazing how everybody gets louder as they drink and it wasn't long before they were all shouting and laughing. When dad went for a refill the whisky bottle was empty so he had to settle for vodka. He sat down again and said to Tony, 'I hate this bloody vodka, it always gives me a headache,' and then swallowed half the contents of the glass in one gulp.

It wasn't long before they were all in a similar state as the guns had been, and Michelin Molly wasn't far behind them. She jumped up and shouted, 'Cabaret time!' And then announced, 'I am going to sing you a song titled, I am dancing with tears in my eyes because the girl in my arms is a boy.' She then burst into song. This was followed by Are You Lonesome Tonight and I Will Take You Home Again Kathleen. Dad said to Tony, 'I don't know about Kathleen, but I wish Jennie would come and take me home.'

Molly had stopped singing to pour a drink and the football boys in the corner were arguing and had started pushing each other quite aggressively. The two Rangers' boys had taken a sudden dislike to the Celtic boy and had pushed him up against the wall. Spud was standing behind them grinning and saying, 'Thump the bastard!' The Celtic boy, fearing the worst, took a swing aimed at the nose of one of the Rangers' boys. He saw it coming and ducked and Spud collected the blow plumb on his chin, and was back in his favourite position on the floor again. Molly dived in and dragged them apart, giving them a good telling off. She said, 'Just settle down and shake hands.' They shook hands and Spud was helped to his feet looking quite dazed. Molly said, 'Now have another drink and enjoy yourself.'

Molly carried on with her cabaret act, singing a selection of Christmas Carols as well as more songs. At one stage she even lifted up her long dress six inches, exposing her wellies, to perform some traditional Irish folk dancing.

The picking-up brigade were discussing the day's events and Lionel was complaining bitterly about what Jack had done to his dog. Flash was sitting on a stool wedged in a corner and Wally had just sat next to him after refilling their glasses with the fifth rather large barcardi and coke. Lionel was becoming more agitated and kept turning round and staring at Wally. His friends were encouraging him and saying, 'You go and tell him Lionel.' Wally saw him staring and said, 'What are you looking at fancy pants. Is it time for my lesson?' Lionel stared at Wally who was sitting on the high stool with his enormous belly hanging down past his crutch. He then strolled over like John Wayne and said, 'Yes it is, you fat bastard! I have been doing karate for the last five years and I have been waiting to try it out on someone.'

He then leapt up in the air and shouted something in Japanese. When he landed he was standing just in front of Wally with his hands poised in the air ready for an attack, but looked more like a windmill that had broken down. Wally slowly shuffled off his stool until his feet were on the floor. Then with tremendous speed he delivered the Glasgow kiss with his forehead right onto the bridge of Lionel's nose. Lionel dropped to the ground like a stone and what a mess his face was. There was blood pouring from his nose and the swelling around his eyes was growing by the second. Wally climbed back on his stool and said, 'I'll have to take that karate up myself. It must come in very useful if you get into trouble.'

The atmosphere was now quite electric and even Molly couldn't calm things completely. Within the next five minutes the Celtic boy was beaten up, Spud was sick in the corner, Flash swallowed his last two pills and then collapsed on the floor, Bonnie and Clyde couldn't hold back any longer and started to perform with a live sex show, and then thank goodness, mum arrived to take us home. The two Rangers' boys walked out in front of us and lifted the two cans of lager that they had brought in three hours earlier.

We were in the car when mum said, 'Did you have a good time dear?' To which dad replied, 'No it was bloody awful,' and then he lay back in the seat. A little while later she said, 'That is the only house I know where you have to put your boots on before you go in.' She didn't receive a reply because he had fallen asleep. For someone who doesn't like vodka he had certainly consumed some. And if I know him, he will be back next Christmas for another dose.

CHAPTER 7

The Boxing Day shoot

The syndicate that dad belonged to were mainly a happy bunch most of the time, but a great deal of extracting the urine was the norm, and occasionally somebody would get the hump about it. Whenever this happened it was like fuel for the fire and only encouraged more sarcasm than ever.

Doddy was the name of the man who organised things, and the self-appointed captain. Taking everything into consideration he made a pretty good job of it, not that anybody would tell him that though. In fact they would wind him up by telling him the complete opposite.

They rented the ground from a farmer and his wife for a very modest fee. The farmer liked a shot himself and his wife had a Labrador and enjoyed picking-up with it. The farmer's name was Humphrey, but everybody called him Twiggy because he was built like a stick insect. His wife, Doreen, was the total opposite build and the real outdoor type, with huge breasts and a rugged complexion. Her hair stuck up in all directions and was completely out of control.

The syndicate members generally never bothered with beaters. Instead they would take turns to walk and stand. However, Twiggy and Doreen had a son called Nigel, and although he had no interest whatsoever in shooting, they insisted that he came with a stick and were hoping he would learn to enjoy their way of life.

There were several cottages on the farm and Twiggy had sold one of them to an ex-military man who was called Captain Parker, a move that he has deeply regretted ever since. It turned out that Captain Parker is an anti. He is anti-shooting, anti-hunting, anti-fishing and anti-rambling. Dad reckons he is probably anti-aircraft, antiseptic and anticlockwise as well. He makes life as difficult as he can for the syndicate and interferes all the time. He is a rude and arrogant man who finds it difficult to mind his own business, and it wasn't too long before he was given the name of Nosy, which goes incredibly well with Parker.

The syndicate members included dad with me, Tony with Grob, a man who had been divorced three times and was having problems with his fourth marriage, who the members affectionately call

Lovelost. He has two golden retrievers called Janice and Janet that are inseparable. Doddy, who has a black Labrador dog which is incredibly randy. There is Mick the Irishman who has the Irish water spaniel called Paddy and the other three members consist of a man called Norman who has a German short-haired pointer, snobbish Charles with the Welsh spaniel which we all call Taffy and Disastrous Den with Lulu. Twiggy was not an official member although he and Doreen rarely missed a shoot.

Christmas is a strange time for us dogs! For two weeks before the event, mum and dad were bringing goodies home and putting them in the cupboard until the shelves were overflowing. I like to see all this food coming into the house but they wouldn't let me have any, and what I found even stranger was they didn't eat it themselves. Dad's drinks' cabinet was filling up nicely as he brought home a bottle every other day.

After dark on Christmas Eve they took me to the local village square where there was a gathering of people around a massive Christmas tree. The local band was playing and everybody was singing Christmas Carols. There were lots of children there looking tremendously excited, as though they were expecting something to happen. The two old ladies standing in front of us were saying how nice it was to see the children being so well behaved.

After about an hour the band stopped playing the Carols' music and started to play Jingle Bells. The excitement between the children and their parents was mounting by the second and then all of a sudden Father Christmas appeared. He was dressed in a red robe and had a massive artificial white beard. He staggered out of the local pub, which is situated on the square, carrying a bag of presents for the children, and in their stampede to get to him they nearly knocked over the two old ladies and one of them stood on my tail. Every year Father Christmas comes out of the same pub. There is little wonder that the children are sceptical about the stories of Father Christmas and his reindeer. After all, if it was true then why isn't it tied up outside?

Father Christmas gave out the presents, which were bars of chocolate, and then made a hasty retreat back into the licensed grotto he had just come out from before the greedy little darlings nicked his beard. Then someone else came out with a large container of soup. Mum and dad had some soup with the others and I sat and watched. It's a time of good will to all men, but what about the dogs? Chocolate and soup for them but nothing for me except a flattened tail.

We then went into the pub to find Father Christmas but he had changed into our friendly innkeeper, whose main objective in life is to take as much of dad's hard-earned money as he can and give him liquid in return.

This was the start of Christmas for us. They had several drinks and I had a bag of crisps. There were other people in the grotto who had obviously decided on an early start for Christmas, and although they were having great difficulty in managing to squeeze any more alcohol into themselves, they seemed reluctant to stop trying. The language coming from some of them would have made Paddy sound like a saint.

We headed back home and mum and dad seemed to be in a good mood. When we arrived dad said to mum, 'Let's have a Christmas drink,' and went straight over to the drinks' cabinet. He must have forgotten that they had just spent two hours in the pub. At midnight they wished each other Merry Christmas, had another drink and then exchanged presents. They tore the wrapping off the presents and what a surprise. Dad had a bottle of whisky and mum a bottle of gin.

On Christmas Day morning mum was busy transferring the goodies she had been storing from the cupboards into bowls and dishes that were placed around the house. Bowls of nuts and fruit. Bags of crisps, tins and boxes of chocolates and biscuits. There was damn near enough to feed an army. She then took out of the fridge a massive bird. I thought to myself, I am glad I wasn't there when he shot that, as I couldn't have picked it up. That went into the oven with half the side of a pig sliced up and placed over it. She then peeled a pan full of potatoes and prepared four different types of vegetables.

At midday dad was standing admiring the contents of his drinks' cabinet when he suddenly announced, 'I'm not keen on drinking at home. I think I will go down the pub for a pint.' Mum said, 'Don't be too long dear, dinner will be ready in two hours.'

When he returned his face had changed colour to a brighter red and he was in a good mood. Mum said to him, 'I'm afraid the turkey is nowhere near ready, so dinner is going to be late.' He replied, 'Not to worry! I will have a drink while I'm waiting,' and was into the cabinet within seconds. Not too bad for someone who had only declared two hours earlier that he wasn't keen on drinking at home.

He doesn't get nasty when he is drinking, in fact he is quite the opposite, always stroking me and telling me I am a good girl. The only thing that bothers me is he wobbles a bit when he takes me for a walk, and I am frightened he might fall on top of me.

An hour and a few drinks later mum called him into the dining room for Christmas dinner. The plates were piled high with so much food it was ridiculous. And just in case that there wasn't enough on the plates the turkey was in the centre of the table. There were two bottles of wine on the table and the drinking started again. It all went very quiet as they got stuck into their feast, with a momentary break to pull a cracker. I knew they would never eat it all and waited patiently for my turn.

Sure enough I ended up with as much as them and Christmas night I had another large portion of turkey. I really enjoyed it but it had an adverse effect on my stomach creating lots of wind. Well, better out than in I thought and just let it go at will. After accusing mum of making the smell dad soon realised the source of the problem and took me out for a walk. We met a dog who lives nearby suffering from the same problem as me and we farted in harmony as we walked past each other.

They never stopped eating and drinking until midnight and yet they had made no impression on the heap of food that was stacked around the house. Eventually they went to bed and I lay in my basket. I certainly didn't need the central heating turned on because I had my own supply of constant hot air. Shame about the smell though!

Boxing Day morning and I was still farting away when they came down stairs. They couldn't really complain though because they were suffering the same fate. He looked a bit rough after indulging the day before but that didn't stop him from filling a hip flask with whisky for later. We had a light breakfast of cold turkey and mum prepared the packed lunch of cold turkey sandwiches. I think he was fed up of the sight of the turkey already because he kept tearing great lumps off it and giving them to me. I knew it was going to create another load of wind but I wasn't going to miss out on his generosity.

On the way to the shoot he had the car window open all of the way. When he broke wind it was quite noisy, which gave me an indication of what was to follow and I could hold my breath until it had cleared. When I broke wind it was silent but deadly and caught him out every time. I found it quite amusing as he would say, 'Bloody hell Bess! You could give some warning,' and then blasted away again himself as though he was demonstrating how.

We arrived at the farm in plenty of time. There were quite a few of them there already and they all looked as rough as dad did. They were telling each other how much they had eaten and drunk the day before as though it was a competition. One thing was for certain, they were all suffering from the windy turkey syndrome.

Tony had invited The Greg as a guest. He is an enormous man who has a beard a bit like Father Christmas, only red. A rugged looking character who says what he thinks, without worrying too much about the consequences. A lot of people don't like him but dad and Tony do, and they often went on wildfowling trips with him. He liked to drink gin but his light blue eyes always turned pink when he had drunk a few, just like an albino.

Most of them had arrived now and were getting ready. Twiggy had with him the reluctant Nigel and informed the others that his wife, Doreen, would be coming a little later and would just go to the first drive to pick up and see them there.

Disastrous Den had a new gun for Christmas and was carefully putting it together. Everyone was waiting for him to drop it. Charles had bought himself some new clothes and was walking up and down showing them off like a model. He had a look-alike tweed jacket. It was obvious that it was a very cheap version as the plastic lining gave it away. To accompany this was a new green peaked cap with pull down flaps for the ears, it looked like something surplus to requirements from the Russian army. He had on new blue waterproof trousers, an extremely bright yellow tie, and to complement everything he was wearing dark sunglasses. Tony said to dad, 'Just look at Charles with his new outfit. Doesn't he look a prat? I'll bet they were cheap. Everything he buys is rubbish.'

Lulu came running over to me and said, 'Hi Bess, did you have a good day yesterday?' I replied, 'Yes it was good, but I have probably eaten too much turkey because I have been farting ever since, and he has just given me a lot more this morning.' Lulu replied, 'Thanks for letting me know, I will keep upwind of you.'

Paddy came across and joined us and said, 'Isn't this fecking Christmas a carry on?' I replied, 'How do you mean Paddy?' He said, 'Listen to me now and I will tell you. On Christmas Eve my dad wanted to go to Midnight Mass. His conscience always seems to bother him at this time of the year. He was like a bear with a sore head before it though, because my mum had started drinking at eight o'clock and he couldn't have one. My mum told him to have one anyway, and that the priest wouldn't notice because he would be probably stinking of drink himself. But he was adamant. He insisted that Christmas was a time for religion and not an excuse to get pissed.

'Well, he went to Midnight Mass to a church that was called something like The Immaculate Contraption. But the bastard took me with him and I had to sit in the car outside in the cold. After it was over he got into the car, but before he had a chance to drive away the priest tapped on the window and asked, 'Would you like to join me and a few friends for a Christmas drink and a turkey salad buffet in my house?' We drove round the back of the church to the priest's house and the bastard left me again.

'Two hours later when he came out he was unable to stand unaided. Someone had called a taxi and with considerable difficulty they managed to dump him in the front seat of it, tucking his unworkable legs in last. They then let me out of his car and I jumped into the taxi and was sitting on the floor between his legs. I don't think he even knew that I was there. After slamming the door the Good Samaritans went back into the priest's house to continue with their piss up.

'The driver asked dad, 'Where to mate?' There was no response from my dad. The driver asked again, 'Where do you want to go mate?' And still no response. The driver shone his torch on dad's face and said, 'Are you all right mate?' I looked at his face in the torch light and could see that he certainly was not. His face was as white as a sheet and his bottom lip was hanging down dribbling saliva. He then slurred, 'I zinc am gonna be zick!' The driver was horrified and shouted, 'Oh no! Not in here mate!' His desperate plea was in vain as I saw the regurgitated, partially digested turkey salad buffet, heading towards me through the beam of the torch. It was accompanied and encouraged in its flow by the liquid content, which consisted of an estimated ten cans of McEwans Export. If I know him this would have been blended with plenty of whisky and complemented by half a dozen brandy and port chasers. Obviously this was the cause of the eruption and for the following minute the bastard pebble-dashed me.

'Not surprisingly the driver was extremely angry and leapt out of the taxi. Coming round to the near side he opened the door and dragged my dad out onto the pavement. He then thought of dragging me out until he saw the state of my coat. I jumped out and shook some of the bigger lumps off transferring them onto the side of the taxi. The driver shouted, 'You are both as bad as each other,' and then he jumped into his taxi and sped off.'

Lulu was laughing while listening as she said, 'What happened next Paddy?' He carried on saying, 'Well, it didn't get a lot better. He just lay there on the pavement for five minutes and then must have decided it was time to get up. It took him five attempts to stand and then after taking three steps sideways he was down again in a heap. While this performance was going on it started raining, which was quite handy as it helped to wash some of the stickier bits of his meal off my coat.

'Several more determined attempts and he was up again and setting off on the mile walk home, supported by his very rubbery legs. Well, he was improving as he made twenty yards before he changed direction sharply to the right where he tripped over a low garden wall and flattened three rose bushes before he stopped rolling. After lying there for five minutes he crawled back onto the pavement on his hands and knees.

'They say practice makes perfect and I will give him his due he was trying hard. He was actually going quite well at one stage until he took a liking to a privet hedge and dived sideways into it. Not surprisingly he seemed to find it considerably more difficult scrambling out of the hedge than he had diving in. Eventually he clambered out and took five consecutive side-steps to the left before crashing into a lamppost. The lamppost provided good support for a while and he hung onto it until he regained his composure.

'After several deep breaths and a shake of the head he was off again, with four steps to the right and two to the left, but not necessarily in that order. A man came round the corner and was walking a dog towards us. I could see the horror on the man's face as he had to decide which side he was going to try and pass this staggering drunk in front of him. He made his choice and went to the left side. Unfortunately, the dog went to the right and dad tripped over the dog's lead and was back down again in a heap on the pavement. The man tried to help dad to his feet but he repaid this kindness by trying to pebble-dash his dog. He missed the dog but the splash back from the pavement provided quite a nice mosaic pattern on the man's shoes, which did not impress him at all.

'We eventually arrived home and I think he would have announced his arrival better had he opened the gate instead of doing a forward roll over it. He pulled himself together again and staggered along the garden path. As he went to lean on the front door mum opened it. He took two more staggering steps forward and fell on the floor of the hall. Mum slammed the front door and shouted at me to get into my basket. She then went upstairs leaving him lying there. Ten seconds later he was asleep.

'Early in the morning he woke and sat up, leaning against the wall. He looked around and saw me looking at him from my basket. He smiled and said, 'Merry Christmas Paddy.' Wonderful, I thought. There's me with half of his cold turkey salad supper, garnished with a whisky, beer and brandy dressing, still stuck in my coat and all he can say is Merry Christmas.'

I said, 'Bugger me Paddy! What an experience, are you all right now?' He replied, 'I will be when they shoot the duck pond later and I can have a swim. I have still got some bits of carrot and tomato skin in my coat. It's amazing how they are always there, isn't it?'

Janice and Janet, the two retrievers, were running around the farmyard side by side. The way they moved they looked as though they were joined together.

Doddy started organising things and they drew to see who was to be a standing gun and who was to be a walking gun on the first drive. Tony, dad, Charles, Den, and Mick were to walk, so the rest of them went to stand at the other end of the wood. I wandered over to Taffy and said, 'This should be more interesting for you than the wildfowling Taffy.' He replied, 'Yes I suppose so, but he won't hit any pheasants. It's not just the ducks he misses, it's everything. Just look at him now, prancing around in his new clothes. He's had them on in the house for the last three days.'

Doddy blew the whistle and we started. There weren't a lot of pheasants in this particular wood and the ones that were there were hard to move. For some reason they didn't want to fly, and I even found one with its head stuck down a rabbit hole. Because it couldn't see me it must have thought that I couldn't see it. I gave it a nudge with my nose but it refused to budge. I stood and pointed at it and eventually dad noticed. He came over and pulled it out and then threw it up in the air. It soared out over the trees and took its chances as it flew the gauntlet over the guns. It might have been lucky and found someone like Charles underneath it.

We worked our way through the wood with Grob and me on the right side, Paddy and Lulu on the left and Taffy in the centre next to Nigel. A pheasant got up and turned back, flying right over Charles. He fired the compulsory two barrels and the pheasant flew on. I looked across at Taffy and he was sitting with his front legs in an open gesture. As much as to say, 'What did I tell you?' It wasn't exactly a difficult chance and if Nigel had thrown his stick he would have probably hit the pheasant.

As we approached the end of the wood we came to a ditch with a foot of water in the bottom. I have been in the ditch before and below the water is very soft mud that stinks rotten. Grob flushed a pheasant and instead of flying over the guns it turned back. Dad shot it and it landed in the ditch in front of Charles. Taffy doesn't like getting dirty so he pretended he hadn't seen it and started to hunt in the opposite direction. Before I had a chance to retrieve it Charles decided to go in and get it himself. He stepped into the ditch and immediately sunk in the mud up to his knees. Tony and dad had to pull his arms to help him out and while they were doing so his sunglasses fell off and sunk in the muddy water, never to be seen again. The mud had traveled up inside his trousers and down into his boots. His lovely blue trousers were now a dirty muddy colour up past the knees and he looked horrified. Dad was grinning as he said, 'Thanks for the retrieve but I could have sent the dog.' Charles replied, 'I thought that there was just a little water in the bottom. It's worse than the bloody Ouse Washes.' Tony was quick to say, 'You missed everything there as well if I remember right Charlie.'

Charles was not pleased as we joined the others outside the wood. There were several sarcastic remarks like, 'When did you change your trousers Charles?' And, 'I like the two-tone trousers Charles. Did the smell come with them?' Taffy came over to me and said, 'What a total fool he is, I am so ashamed of him. Oh by the way! Have you smelt Paddy this morning? He stinks of sick.' I replied, 'I know he does, but it isn't his own.'

Doreen had arrived late and was still picking-up. Tony and dad were talking to her husband, Twiggy, when The Greg walked over, and in his usual subtle way he said, 'Who is the bird picking-up with the big tits and the spiky hair?' Dad and Tony looked at each other really shocked, not knowing what to say. Then Twiggy just burst out laughing and said, 'My wife will really appreciate that remark. She is very proud of her chest.' You would think that The Greg would have been embarrassed but he just said, 'So she should be. It's a beauty!'

We all set off walking to the next drive and Lulu was alongside me chattering away. She said, 'Where I live Bess the back garden gate leads straight out onto the downs and that is where he trains me. There are lots of rabbits and he makes me sit and watch them. It is so boring and the rabbits just laugh at me because they know I am not allowed to chase them. Well, last night he was drunk when he took me for a walk and when we returned, not only did he not close the kennel door properly, but he also left the garden gate open. I looked out of the gate and the rabbits were out there enjoying themselves. I can tell you this Bess, they won't laugh at me again. I spent hours chasing them until there wasn't a rabbit left above the ground. It's a pity you were not with me Bess, because if we had worked together we could have caught a few.' I replied, 'I would have enjoyed that Lulu. I never get the chance to chase anything. Some dogs even chase their tail in frustration but I had mine docked when I was a week old. They only left four inches but it is amazing how many people manage to stand on it when I am sitting. I remember the man docking it. He said it wouldn't hurt, but it did.' Lulu said, 'The same thing happened to me. I have always found that if ever they tell you it's not going to hurt you can bet your life it will. I notice that they never cut pieces off each other.' I replied, 'I believe the Jews have been known to on occasions with circumcision of young males.' Lulu pulled a face and said, 'That sounds worse than losing your tail.'

The next drive was to be Tawny Wood. This is without a doubt the best drive on the shoot. Doddy was telling everyone that he had been in the wood earlier and fed the birds. He had said that there were about one hundred pheasants in and around the pen.

We were walking to position and about three hundred yards away from the wood when a dozen pheasants flew out. Doddy watched them flying and said, 'Bugger me! What's the matter with them?' As he said it a lot more got up and the cock birds were screeching their warning calls. Doddy looked horrified and said, 'There must be a bloody fox in there.' Then a great big bunch of fifty or more birds flew out. Doddy was furious and said, 'We will shoot the bloody fox. Vince, you take The Greg and walk through the wood. The rest of us will surround it.'

They all took up their position then dad and The Greg started to walk through with me at heel. It was a weird atmosphere in the wood as we were going through. Dad and The Greg were scanning the ground ready to shoot the poor fox. I hate to see foxes shot, as they are very much like us dogs. The only difference is they have to find their own food and everyone hates them. I had a good sniff but I couldn't smell a fox. I found this very strange because I can usually smell one from a quarter of a mile away.

We slowly walked on and a jay flew across in front of dad. It was lucky because dad let it go, no doubt hoping for something to jump up with four legs and a bushy tail. I could have told him that wasn't going to happen.

As we approached the pen there wasn't a pheasant in sight but I saw some movement inside the pen. Dad and The Greg didn't appear to have seen anything but I knew that I had seen something move behind some straw bales. I wasn't sure what it was, although I knew it wasn't a fox.

Dad walked down one side of the pen and The Greg walked down the other side. I went in through the pen door, which was open, and dad shouted at me to come back. I was determined to find out what the movement was and decided to ignore him and have a look.

I ran up to the bales and there lying in behind them was Nosy Parker. I barked at him as loud as I could and made the hair on my back stand up to try and frighten him. Dad and The Greg came running into the pen and Nosy stood up and said, 'Okay, you have caught me but the pheasants have gone and you won't shoot the poor things today.' The Greg said to him, 'You righteous bastard! What right have you got to ruin our day?' He replied smugly, 'What right have you got to murder the pheasants?' Dad looked really angry and said, 'Unlike you we don't get a pension paid for by the tax payers for playing tin soldiers for thirty years. We live in the real world and have to work to earn our money. We choose to use that money to rent the shoot here. We buy in the pheasant poults and rear them. We protect them against predators and feed them on the best of food. We look after them better than some people look after their children. What we do is law abiding and that is what gives us the right to shoot.' Nosy replied with a grin, 'You might think you have the right but the pheasants have gone now.' The Greg isn't one to mince words. He took the cartridges out of his gun and passed it to dad. He then said, 'If we can't have some sport with the pheasants pal, we will have some with you.' Nosy stopped grinning and said, 'Don't you try and mix it with me sonny. I was in the army for thirty years.' The Greg replied, 'I don't give a shit if you were in the bloody air force and the navy as well, you are coming with me.' He then grabbed hold of Nosy and held him in a headlock. He walked him out of the pen and through the wood and all Nosy could do was wave his arms a bit.

We came out at the side of the wood and when the others saw us they came across to us. The Greg said, 'Here is your bloody fox,' and released his hold. Nosy looked frightened and said, 'I will have you done for assault.' The Greg replied, 'Well in that case I had better assault you properly,' and lifted his fist in the air as though he was going to thump him. Nosy put his hands over his face and cowered. Twiggy said, 'What a lousy thing to do Mr. Parker. I know you are anti-shooting but you should respect other peoples' rights. The two fields next to your house will have the shit spreader in tomorrow, and every day after that for a fortnight. That will teach you not to interfere. Now clear off!' Nosy walked away looking really shaken.

They decided that it was lunch time and we all went back to the farmyard. Dad was walking with The Greg when Doreen joined them. She put her arm inside The Greg's and squeezed her chest tight against him as she said, 'I like big strong men like you.' The Greg smiled and said, 'Well that's fine because I like a woman with big tits.' Dad looked embarrassed again but Doreen just laughed and replied, 'I think we are going to get on well.'

We had our lunch in a barn that was spotless. Quite a contrast to some of the places where we go beating! Everyone was trying to give each other their turkey sandwiches and it was a good day for the dogs. I will never understand why they all buy a great big turkey when most of them don't even like it.

The two inseparable retrievers, Janice and Janet, were being fed with turkey sandwiches. Lovelost was breaking pieces off and passing them down under the table to them. I heard Janice say, 'You have that piece Janet.' Janet replied, 'Oh no, you have it, I had the last one.' Then Janice said, 'But the last one was just a small one so I don't mind if you have that one as well.' Janet replied, 'I still think that you should have it Janice.' Grob was sitting close by and grabbed it out of Lovelost's hand. He quickly swallowed it and said, 'That settled that disagreement. If you need any more help just shout.' Paddy said to me, 'Jeezus! Them three make a fine pair if ever I saw one.'

After they all had a boring conversation about whose turkey was the moistest, the drinks came out. Each one of them had either a hip flask or a bottle and it started to flow. Grob said to me, 'If this lunch time drink is anything like last year, that will be the end of the shooting for the day.'

Half an hour later a policeman walked into the barn and Grob started to growl. I said, 'What's the matter Grob, don't you like them?' He replied, 'I don't know why but I bloody hate them.' The policeman sidestepped Grob and said to Twiggy, 'I have been looking for you, I have had a complaint.' Twiggy replied with a smile, 'What kind of a complaint officer?' The policeman looked around at everyone and he seemed very uncomfortable as he said, 'Someone claims that he has been assaulted by one of your team.' Doreen walked over to the policeman. Moving extremely close and pushing her chest into him she said, 'That must be Nosy Parker. He was trespassing in our wood causing criminal damage. He was escorted out of the wood for his own safety.' The poor policeman looked even more uncomfortable now with Doreen's chest tight against him and he took a step backwards before he said, 'That's not what he told me.' She stepped forward to regain her original position and said quite firmly, 'I don't give a toss what that little shit told you. I have told you what happened and everyone in here saw it.' She then walked across the barn and lifted a brace of pheasants that were hanging on a hook. Walking back to him she said, 'Would you like a brace of pheasants officer?' He looked at the pheasants and replied, 'They are not a bribe are they?' She looked at them herself and said, 'They look like a brace of pheasants to me. Do you want them or not?' He thought for a moment and said, 'Yes please,' as he took them off her. He then walked out of the barn as Grob growled at him again. When he had gone she said to Twiggy, 'Put the shit spreader in the fields next to Nosy's house for four weeks, never mind two, and spread some on Nosy as well if you get the chance.'

They spent quite a while drinking and laughing but nobody seemed to have had too much, and The Greg's eyes had only turned slightly pink, so they decided to shoot the duck pond and then call it a day. They had reared one hundred and fifty mallard this season which were in prime condition.

The pond is a natural dip in the ground fed by a small watercourse and there are plenty of trees and bushes around it to give shelter. The way it is shot is quite different to most ponds. The guns stand in a curve about two hundred yards back from it and the ducks are driven off the pond. They always fly out the same way and if they are a good height when they go over the guns they will have a shot. More often than not the ducks come off a bit too low and the guns let them pass. They fly down to the end of the valley gaining height all the way. They then generally turn and head back towards the pond. When they are returning they are high birds that are really moving. That is when they have a shot at them. Some of the ducks will fly back out again giving a second chance.

The guns were in position and Doreen and Nigel approached the pond from the opposite side waving bags. The ducks came off in one massive bunch heading straight towards us. They were barely twenty yards high as they passed over the guns. Nobody put their gun up except Charles. He let rip with both barrels and as usual completely missed. I looked across at Taffy and he was shaking his head in disgust.

The ducks gained height and headed down the valley, splitting up into small bunches as they went. When they returned they passed over the guns and the proper shooting started. As a bunch came over dad he said to me, 'I think they are a bit too high Bess,' and didn't lift his gun. Tony took one out of the same bunch stone dead. Dad then realised that they were not too high and fired a shot himself but missed. He did manage one out of the next bunch and Tony took two. After about ten minutes a dozen ducks had been shot and the rest of the ducks had realised what was happening and were moving to a safer place.

As the last bunch passed over Lovelost he shot one but just winged it. I watched it heading downwards and it landed in the watercourse about three hundred yards away. I looked at dad while waiting for the word and he said, 'Get on!' At the same time Den sent Lulu and we were running flat out across the field to where the duck had gone down. Lulu said, 'I will race you there Bess.' I was going as fast as I could but I couldn't lose her. When we reached the watercourse she went straight in and started hunting to the left. I went to the right because that was the way the water was flowing and I guessed that the duck would want to try and return to the pond. I soon picked up the scent and followed it along the bank. It suddenly became stronger and when I pushed my head under a bunch of brambles the duck was there. I picked it up and headed back across the field to dad. It was twice the weight of any pheasant I have ever picked. Lulu was back alongside me and said, 'You lucky sod Bess.' I knew that there was more than luck involved with that retrieve but I couldn't say anything because my mouth was full of mallard.

That was the end of the day's shooting. They all had another drink and shook each other's hand. Doreen gave everyone a kiss and The Greg received an extra long one. Twiggy pretended that he hadn't noticed and everyone left in a good mood.

When we arrived home mum was pleased to see us. She gave me a bath and I thought of Paddy and his smelly coat. After the bath the eating and drinking started all over again.

After two weeks with the three of us eating to capacity mum threw the rest of the Christmas food store away. Dad told me we had to build up our strength because we would need it on our trip to Scotland. He was going goose shooting in a few days and I was going with him.

CHAPTER 8

Geese on Wigtown Bay

I was looking forward to my trip to Scotland, and even though dad had been several times before, so was he. The atmosphere was great while he was getting all his gear ready and mum was packing things for him. The forecast was for snow up north so the thermals were going into the case. I don't think he could manage without mum, as his memory is terrible. He would leave half the things behind that were needed. That would put him in a bad mood and he would no doubt take it out on me.

Tony and The Greg were coming with us and of course Grob. The Greg had managed to acquire a large Jeep for the journey that belonged to his boss. Apparently, his boss had gone on a skiing holiday and The Greg had found the keys in his boss's desk.

Six o'clock in the morning and The Greg pulled up outside our house in the Jeep. It was still very dark and most of the people who live in the street would be asleep in bed. Not for long though as The Greg announced his arrival with three prolonged blasts on the horn. Dad ran out and told him to be quiet but he just laughed and blasted it again. They loaded all the gear in the Jeep and mum gave me a cuddle and said to dad, 'Don't you work Bess too hard!' Mum wanted to give dad a cuddle too, but because The Greg was there he wouldn't let her. We were then on our way to collect Tony and Grob.

Forty minutes later we were at Tony's house. His neighbours received the same treatment with the horn but it was somewhat later than before. I was sitting on the back seat and Grob jumped in. He was about to go in for a sniff when I said, 'Don't even think about it Grob!' He replied, 'Okay Bess. Are you looking forward to this trip?' I said, 'Yes, but I have never been with him for geese so I don't really know what to expect.' Grob replied, 'It can be great fun but unfortunately it will be very cold. It's all right for them as they wrap up, but we just have the same coat and no warm boots.'

I had heard dad talking to mum when he was booking the accommodation. He told her that he was fed up with staying in dodgy guest-houses so he was booking them into a pub this time. I remember thinking, that should be interesting with him and The Greg together.

It was a long journey up the A1 and Grob snored all the way. It started to snow as we were driving over the high ground on the A66 but cleared as we dropped down the other side. We eventually pulled up in the Jeep outside a pub in a village not far from Wigtown Bay. Dad said, 'We had better go in and make ourselves known.' They walked into the pub and left Grob and I sitting on the back seat. I was bursting for a wee but all he can think about is his bloody beer.

Half an hour later he did come out just as I was about to do it. He opened the door and said, 'Come on you two.' I leapt out and found a grass verge just in time. It was a long wee and all the time he was saying, 'Come on Bess, hurry up it is cold out here.' I was thinking, It might be cold out here but if he had been any longer it would have been wet and smelly in the Jeep.

We walked inside and there was a warm atmosphere in there. A log fire was burning halfway up the chimney and there was a black Labrador dog lying in front of it. He saw us come in and walked across. He smiled at me and said, 'Hello you.' I replied, 'Hi, my name is Bess.' Grob jumped in between us with his hackles up and said, 'Piss off, she is with me.' The landlord was behind the bar and he shouted, 'Get back over there Sam,' and pointed to the fire. Sam turned and walked back lying down again. I said to Grob, 'Every time I try to make friends with a dog you always stick your nose in and spoil it. I have told you before Grob I am not with you.' He replied, 'I am only trying to look after you.'

The landlord's name was Tommy. He had a strong Scottish accent and was a very jovial person who laughed out loud a lot. Everyone seemed to be getting on fine and dad already had the makings of a stupid grin. After a while Tommy's wife came into the bar and he introduced her as Sheila. She had with her a French poodle dog that had been recently cut with the fancy legs and the pompom on its head and on the end of its tail. It looked absolutely ridiculous. Grob immediately said to me, ' Will you take a look at that puffta over there?' Sheila said to the poodle, 'Timmy, go and sit with Sam,' The poodle walked over and sat in front of the fire looking rather embarrassed. Grob shouted, 'Mind you don't burn your pompom darling.' Sam stood up and said quite aggressively, 'You leave him alone. It's not his fault that they cut his coat like that.' Grob was about to go over but I said, 'Leave them alone Grob. I don't want any trouble.' Grob reluctantly stopped and Sam lay down again.

Tommy was a shooting man and dad, Tony and The Greg seemed to like talking to him. From what he was saying he was more into deer stalking than goose shooting and there were quite a few trophies hanging on the wall of the bar.

A couple of pints later and Sheila showed us to a bedroom. It was a warm spacious room with three single beds and an en-suite shower. She said to them, 'I hope you will be comfortable and there are some old bed covers I have put in the corner. They will do for the dogs to sleep on.' I looked around and couldn't believe my luck. I thought Grob and I would have been put out in a cold shed and I would have spent half the night fighting him off. I will probably still have to do that but at least I am going to be warm and comfortable and close to dad.

Grob and I were fed and they all had a shower and changed. We then went back down into the bar where they were served their dinner. The plates were heaped up with meat pie and all the things that go with it. Grob and I were given a lot of it and it certainly tasted much better than the dry rubbish they had given us for our dinner.

After dinner a map was opened up on the bar and Tommy was marking places on the foreshore where he thought it would be best for geese. Dad said to Tommy, 'I appreciate that you are showing us these places, but how do we get to them without crossing farmer's fields? I have had many difficulties with farmers before.' Tommy replied, 'No problem! You decide now where you want to go in the morning and I will ring up the farmer and tell him that you will be there.' They had another discussion about wind and tide and a few other things that I didn't understand and then they picked a place. Tommy was on the phone for a couple of minutes and I heard him say. 'Hello old pal! It is Tommy from the pub. I have three shooters staying and they want to cross your fields in the morning to get to the foreshore.' There was a short pause and then he said, 'Thanks old pal. I will see you later!' He came back and said, 'No problem at all boys. No problem.' Dad said to Tony, 'This is the best place I have ever stayed in.' Tony replied, 'Let's be honest Vince. The places where we have stayed before wouldn't take a lot of beating.'

There were a couple of girls in their early twenties also staying at the pub. They were not chasing geese about but were on a catering course at the nearby college. The Greg was chatting them up and buying them drinks.

The place was starting to fill up and Sheila joined Tommy behind the bar. Everyone that came in got the same greeting from Tommy, 'Hello old pal! How are you?' It was a really friendly place, apart from the fact that Sam and Grob were eyeing each other up again.

About ten-thirty a man came in and after the initial greeting from Tommy he was talking to him at the bar. This man had a disgusting habit of scratching his backside. Most of the time he was scratching and pulling at his trousers around his bum as though his backside was trying to swallow them. Tony said to dad, 'I know how he feels. It is difficult to get to the itch through trousers, long johns and underpants.'

The Greg was now sitting at the table with the two girls. His eyes were rapidly turning pink and he was enjoying himself. He went to the bar to buy more drinks and as he walked past the man who was still scratching he said, 'Have you got a tooth coming through mate?' The man turned away from Tommy and glared at The Greg. Before anything else was said, Tommy said to The Greg, 'Let me introduce you to Jock. He is the farmer whose fields you will be crossing in the morning.' Jock looked angry and said, 'Correction Tommy. I am the farmer whose fields he will not be crossing in the morning.' He then drank the rest of his pint in one swallow, slammed the empty glass on the bar and walked out. Tommy started laughing loudly and couldn't stop. Tony said, 'Here we go! I thought things were going too well.'

The map was back out on the bar and they selected another venue. Tommy was on the phone again to a different farmer and made the necessary arrangements. Dad said to The Greg. 'For Pete's sake, keep your bloody mouth shut.' The Greg replied, 'Bollocks to him! If he had carried on picking at his arse much longer he might have found his brains.' Tommy looked at dad and said, 'Don't worry about it, he will be all right tomorrow night. He often gets in silly moods but they never last. Anyway, he has got to come in here because he has been barred from the other two pubs in the village for scratching his arse.' He then burst out laughing again.

At eleven o'clock the two girls went to their room despite strenuous efforts from The Greg to persuade them to have another drink. Dad looked tired after the journey and it wasn't long before we were all in our room as well. Dad put some blankets next to his bed and I lay on them. It had been a long day and I was ready for some sleep. I was thinking that I would like to get to know Sam if Grob would give me a chance. I was about to go to sleep when I felt Grob's tongue licking my ear. I said, 'Bugger off Grob! I have a headache.' He replied, 'I have got the message,' and walked over to the other side of the room where Tony had put some blankets for him.

It seemed as though I had only just closed my eyes when dad was on the move. He said, 'Come on boys, time to get up and try and be quiet as it is only six o'clock.' The Greg went into the shower and sang one of his dirty rugby songs at his usual volume. There was an electric toaster in the room and tea making facilities. They had tea and toast and then we were in the Jeep and on our way.

It was very cold but not snowing, although there had been some snow overnight but it hadn't really settled. Dad opened the map and gave directions to The Greg as they went. We pulled off the road and onto a track. When we came to a farm gate The Greg drove the Jeep off the track and parked on the grass verge. This was as far as we were driving and we all got out.

It was a cutting wind and they started to put on their extra clothing. Soon we were going through the gate and across the field. Tony shone his torch around the field and I could see a cow in the beam. Tony said, 'I hate them bloody things,' and he started running. The Greg laughed and said, 'The cow won't hurt you Tony, it's her boyfriend you want to look out for.'

When we arrived at the other side of the field we worked our way along the fence until we came to a gate. When we were halfway across the next field dad suddenly said, 'Stop and listen!' The Greg said, 'What's wrong, is the bull coming?' Tony was on the move again and dad said, 'There's no bull Tony, just stop and listen,' He stopped and then I heard the sound of geese. It was a long way away but it was definitely geese chattering to each other. Dad said, 'They are roosting out there. We will have to be quiet from now on and turn out the torch.' Grob said to me, 'This is a good sign Bess. We may be in luck this morning.' I asked, 'How heavy are the geese Grob?' He replied, 'The greylags can be quite heavy and sometimes I have had to drag them back, but those geese out there sound like pinkfeet to me and they are not too heavy. Maybe about six or seven pounds.' I was becoming quite excited now and couldn't wait to retrieve my first goose.

We were going along almost silently and even The Greg was quiet apart from the odd fart. We went through another gate and dad said, 'That should be the last one.' It was still pitch black and we set off again. After about fifty yards of rough grass we walked onto mud and that was my introduction to the foreshore of Wigtown Bay. Tony said, 'The tide is out and not due to start coming in for three hours so we can walk out if we want. Dad replied, 'We might as well because the closer we get to their roost the more chance there will be of them being in range when they come off.'

We were walking for a long time in the mud and it was becoming stickier as we went. Dad was sweating from the effort and leaking a pint of beer every five minutes. First off was the jacket and a while later the thick jumper.

The sound of the geese was much louder now and dad whispered, 'I think we had better stop.' They spread out about fifty yards apart getting in gullies for cover with The Greg on dad's left and Tony left of him. That way there was a dog on each end of the line.

If my mum could have seen me now she would have cried. I was covered in slimy mud all over. The gully we were in was not very deep but a large piece of driftwood had come to rest on the edge of it and we used this for cover. Dad wedged a piece of wood across the gully and sat on it and it wasn't long before the jumper and coat were being put back on. He looked at me next to him and I wagged my tail. He went to stroke me but quickly changed his mind when he felt the state of my coat.

We were waiting a long time and the geese never stopped chattering. We could see the headlights of the vehicles driving on the road at the other side of the bay and dad said, 'Look at them poor sods Bess. They are going to work!'

At the first sign of light a flock of gulls came over us no more than five yards up. They appeared so quickly they made me jump. Dad said quietly, ' Settle down Bess. There will be lots of them.' He was right. There were several more large flocks heading inland and they seemed totally oblivious to our presence. Soon there were teal flying back towards the water and although they were well in range nobody shot at them.

A couple of curlew announced the break of day and once it started to break it seemed to happen very quickly. The first bunch of geese rose with a clamour forming a skein. They were still a long way from us and looked quite small. Dad started to call them with some calls that sounded nothing like that of a goose. I could see he was getting excited and so was I. The geese seemed to react to dad's strange call and turned towards us. He said, 'This could be it Bess,' and started calling again.

While the geese were heading our way several more geese lifted behind them in separate bunches forming a row of skeins. The first skein was getting really close now and the noise from them was tremendous. Dad pushed himself tight against the driftwood and told me to stay still. I could see the geese through a gap in the wood and they seemed very lively and were interchanging positions in the skein as though they couldn't make up their minds which position they wanted to be in. When they were about a hundred yards away dad peeped out over the driftwood and said, 'Shit! They are turning away.' They passed us about sixty yards to our right but they were not very high. Dad cursed the luck of the Raw and the following skein passed us in exactly the same place.

There were more coming with two skeins almost side by side. They were heading on the same flight line until Tony called from the other side. The skeins turned immediately and were then heading towards us. Dad looked at me and whispered, 'Stay still!' A little while later the geese were over the top of us and what a sight it was. The Greg fired first and took one out of the front of the skein which just plummeted down. Then dad and Tony fired almost together. Tony had two birds dead in the air almost side by side. Dad killed one with his first barrel but wing tipped one with his second, which glided down way behind us. The rest of the geese that were following climbed steeply while turning away and screaming their warning calls.

I stared at dad waiting for the command as I was desperate for a retrieve. He had a good look around the sky and then said, 'Get on!' I scrambled up the mud at the side of the gully and started looking for the geese. I could see Grob out as well working away with his nose almost on the mud. I found the goose that dad had shot just lying in the mud with its wings spread. When I picked it up I was surprised how light it was, although one of its wings completely blocked my vision. It was not much heavier than the mallard on the syndicate pond but more difficult to carry. I delivered it to dad after tumbling into the gully and was then out again looking for the one The Greg had shot. I found it after a while at the bottom of a gully. It was lying differently and I got hold of it on its breast. I took it back as well and couldn't stop wagging my tail. That was without doubt one of the most exciting moments in my life.

We stayed for another half-hour and then we were walking back. There was a goose down somewhere and Grob and I were trying to find it. We hunted all the gullies but there was no sign of it and no scent. When we reached the end of the mud we hunted the strip of rough grass. It was there that I picked up the scent and started to hunt along the fence. Suddenly I saw it tucked in next to a clump of grass. As I went to get hold of it, it jumped up and started running and flapping its wings. Grob was coming the other way and grabbed it. Tony quickly dispatched it and everyone was very pleased. (But maybe not the goose.)

There was a burn running close to where the Jeep was parked and Grob and I were given a good wash. The water was absolutely freezing and compared to the water in the burn, the mud on the foreshore was quite warm.

When we arrived back in the pub car park Tommy came out to see us and he had Sam with him. Grob started to look angry again and started growling so Tony put him back in the Jeep. Tommy said to dad, 'How did you get on old pal?' Dad replied. 'We did okay! We were lucky though because we managed to find where they were roosting.' Tommy then said, 'Come on in and tell me about the flight over breakfast.' As we were walking into the pub I looked back at Grob sitting in the Jeep. If looks could kill we would all have perished there and then.

When we walked into the bar I sat next to Sam in front of the fire and he said to me, 'I didn't mean to cause trouble last night Bess.' I replied, 'You didn't Sam. It was Grob. He is always like that when he is with me. He thinks he owns me, but he doesn't.' He then said, 'You are soaking wet girl. I bet they have put you in a burn.' I replied, 'Bloody right they did and it was freezing.' He then asked, 'Did you enjoy yourself this morning?' I replied, 'It was great. That was my first time out for geese and I had two retrieves and I found a runner.' I then asked him, 'Do you go out for the geese with Tommy?' He replied, 'Sometimes, but not very often. He spends most of his time shooting deer and I go with him.' I said, 'They are a bit large to retrieve aren't they.' He smiled and replied, 'Are you taking the piss Bess?' I said, 'No. I know nothing about deer shooting.' He then said, 'Well, he stalks them first and we have to be very quiet while he gets into a position for a safe shot. Then when he shoots them they often run into the undergrowth before they fall over dead. My job is to find them for him. If they are not too big I drag them out for him.' I asked, 'Do you enjoy it?' He replied, 'Yes I do. It's better than getting covered in mud and then being thrown into a freezing cold burn for a wash. But what I enjoy the most though is lying in front of the fire in the bar on an evening while listening to the visiting wildfowlers and stalkers telling their stories. You should hear some of the lies.'

Sheila served the men with breakfast and gave Sam and me a sausage as well. When she put the plate of food in front of The Greg she said to him, 'I have taken the fuse out of the electric shower in your room. If the water is cold you might not be inclined to sing so loud early in the morning.' Dad and Tony looked embarrassed but The Greg just smiled and started eating. Nothing ever seems to bother him.

After breakfast we went out on a reconnaissance ride to try and find where the geese were feeding. When I jumped into the Jeep Grob started sniffing around my mouth and he knew I had eaten a sausage. 'Bloody marvellous!' He said, 'What about me? 'It's your own fault,' I said, 'You shouldn't be so aggressive.' He replied, 'I'll bet that bloody Sam got a sausage as well.' I said, 'Yes, we both had one while we were sitting in front of the fire.' He stated again, 'Bloody marvellous!' And then went into a sulk.

Tommy had written on a piece of paper the name of a farm where the geese might be. We were driving around for some time and they were having difficulty in finding the farm when dad saw an old man walking his dog. He said to The Greg. 'Pull over and I will ask him where the farm is.' Tony said, 'I'll bet you he is the village idiot. Vince has a knack of picking them out.'

The Jeep stopped and dad jumped out and walked up to the man and said, 'Excuse me. Could you please tell me where Ramsey Farm is?' The man looked at him and replied, 'I can't hear you I am deaf.' Tony started to laugh and said, 'He has done it again.' Not to be put off easily dad held out the piece of paper on which the farm name was written and pointed to it. The man squinted at it and said, 'I can't see very well without my glasses. I am nearly blind.' Dad then shouted really loud, 'How do I get to Ramsey Farm?' The man acknowledged that he had heard him with a smile and a nod and said, 'Oh Ramsey Farm. I wouldn't start from here,' and then he walked on leaving dad standing there with his mouth open. Tony was in hysterics in the Jeep and as dad climbed back in he said, 'You can do the asking next time Tony. It's the same every bloody time.'

We did find Ramsey Farm but there was not a sign of a goose on the fields that we could see from the road. We went back to the place where we had been shooting in the morning for the evening flight to try and intercept the geese going back to their roost for the night. As we were walking out Grob said to me, 'I have been on at least ten evening flights for geese and apart for one exception they have shot nothing. The only time they were successful was under the moon. So don't expect too much Bess.'

We couldn't get out as far as we had been in the morning because the tide was still receding. Dad crouched down into a gully and I sat alongside him. I enjoyed these moments with dad. The waiting always seemed to give me the feeling that we were working as a team. Dad would keep talking to me and I knew he enjoyed my company. I liked to show my affection by snuggling up to him but he wasn't too keen on that when I was covered in mud.

It was nearly dark when the geese returned and dad had stood up. There were three large skeins that flew over us and although we could clearly hear them it was too dark to see them. Their calls were constant as they flew over and I noticed how their calls altered and were quieter as they must have reached their destination.

We were soon heading back without a shot being fired and Grob seemed to be pleased that his prediction had been right. 'Serves them right for not giving me a sausage,' he sniggered. Another good dunking in the freezing cold burn followed by a rub down with a towel and we were on our way back in the Jeep.

It was busy in the bar that night. Sam and Timmy, the French poodle, were sitting by the fire and I wanted to go and join them, but I was frightened that it might make Grob angry and then he would cause trouble. The men were talking about all aspects of country ways and dad told a few stories about ferreting. One of the stories was about a time when the ferret had killed down the hole. It must have had a good feed and decided to sleep next to its victim. Dad dug for hours trying to locate it. He was frightened to leave it because there was a hen run only three hundred yards away and the ferret could have created havoc in there. He managed to dig it out but it was late at night when he found it and he was tired. Tommy said, 'Oh we didn't mess about like that when we were ferreting. We made sure that the ferret couldn't kill underground.' Dad smiled and said, 'And how did you do that Tommy? With a muzzle?' He replied quite seriously, 'No, I don't like muzzles. We pulled their bloody teeth out.' Dad said, 'You must be joking.' 'No I am not,' said Tommy, 'We pulled them out with a pair of pliers. We didn't have time to mess about when we were poaching. A ferret with teeth was no good to us.' Dad was laughing as he said, 'So what did you feed them on?' Tommy grinned and said, 'Rice pudding and porridge, but not too thick, you ken.'

Amongst the people in the bar there were three characters who were salmon poachers. From what Tommy had told dad they netted just about every pool in the area and supplied most of the hotels with fresh salmon. The police knew what they were up to but could never manage to catch them.

One of them was telling a story about a time when they were netting a pool. They usually netted in the dark but this particular time they did it in daylight. The reason for this was they knew that there were some fish in the pool and with the water rising fast the fish might well have moved by night-time. Anyway, one of them was the lookout and he saw a policeman coming from quite a distance away. They had time to hide their nets in some bushes and when the policeman arrived the three of them were stood on the river bridge leaning against the wall while having a smoke. The policeman said to them, 'There has been a report that three suspicious characters have been seen around here today.' One of them replied with a straight face, 'Well, we have been here all morning officer and we haven't seen anyone.' This brought a great roar of laughter from everyone in the bar, which only encouraged more stories.

A while later Jock walked in. Tommy saw him and said, 'Hello old pal!' and pulled a pint for him. Jock stood at the bar for a while and then looked slowly around. The Greg was sitting at a table with the girls and when Jock saw him The Greg smiled and said, 'We are watching you Jock.' He turned away and leant against the bar again. All the time his hand kept coming round towards his backside and then he would remember he was being watched and pull it away again. After about fifteen minutes his itch must have been driving him mad and so he went into the toilet. When he walked back into the bar The Greg shouted, 'I'll bet that feels better now Jock.' He changed direction and walked over to the table where The Greg and the two girls were sitting. It went deadly quiet for a while as Jock stood there glaring at The Greg. The Greg just smiled and stood up. He was six inches taller and four stone heavier than Jock. He then said, 'Don't you dare lay a finger on me Jock. I know where the bloody thing has just been.' Dad was just taking a drink of beer when The Greg spoke and he sprayed the back of Tony's head with the contents of his mouth. The whole pub erupted in laughter again and Jock stormed out leaving his beer on the counter.

The pub was supposed to close at eleven to non-residents but at quarter to twelve the local policeman came in and had a drink. The music was blaring out from the box on the wall and they all seemed to be having a good time. The climax of the evening was when the two girls were dancing on one of the tables and the men stood around clapping their hands. It is just as well mum wasn't with us.

A little while later the girls went to bed and it became much quieter. They started talking about shooting again and someone called Rab mentioned greylags. Dad was very interested to know where the greylags were and bought Rab a pint. It turned out that Rab was a farm worker and he said that there were about fifty greylags that had been feeding on one of their fields for about a week. Dad asked if there was a chance of having a shot at them and Rab told them that the farmer would be pleased to see them frightened away. He drew a map of where to go and that was the plan for the morning.

They were talking again and this time they were discussing collective nouns. Tommy said, 'What do they call a group of crows?' Tony replied straight away, 'A murder.' Tommy said, 'You are not as stupid as you look Tony, that is correct.' He then said, 'Okay, what do they call a group of ravens?' Once again Tony replied, 'I think it is an unkindness,' 'Tommy said, 'Bugger me you are right again.' Dad then asked, 'What is the collective noun for a group of beaters?' Tommy replied quickly, 'A shower of bastards.'

Sheila said, 'I don't know about you lot but I am ready for bed.' She then said, 'Come on Timmy.' The poodle jumped up and walked out of the bar with her. Grob shouted, 'Don't forget to put the curlers in your pompoms darling.' That was the last straw for Sam and he ran across the room and latched onto Grob. Give Grob his due he could mix it with most dogs but by the time they were pulled apart they both had wounds to lick. It was two o'clock when we finally went to bed. In four hours time we would be up again. Grob kept me awake while licking a couple of holes in his leg caused by Sam's teeth.

The alarm went off and dad got out of bed and switched the kettle on. The others started to get up but they didn't look as happy as they had done four hours earlier. The Greg never bothered with his shower and instead of the usual conversation it was mainly burps and farting.

Tommy had told dad that there were some shell decoys in the shed at the back of the pub and dad was trying to find them with the help of a torch, and up to his waist in empty cardboard boxes. There were several curses as he was falling about but he did find some in the end with four crates of empty bottles stacked on top of them. The Greg said, 'I hope the greylags enjoy a drink because the bloody decoys stink of booze'. Tony replied, 'So do you Greg so don't worry about it.' We were then on our way to the farm where the greylags were supposed to be.

I was looking forward to this flight. I had heard about greylags but the thought of retrieving one was something special. Grob was limping really badly after his fight with Sam and Tony decided to leave him in the Jeep. Grob did not look at all pleased, but I was. Call me selfish if you want but I was really looking forward to a retrieve and with Grob not there I knew there would be a better chance for me. Tony is a good shot and if the geese do come he is the one most likely to hit one.

Rab came out of a large shed in the farmyard as dad was getting ready and he explained where we had to go. We walked across several fields and then came to a field where a burn was the boundary along two sides. They started to search the grass with their torches and soon found the evidence they were looking for. A large amount of fresh goose droppings just forty yards away from the edge of the burn and on a slight slope that went down to the burn. There were some small bushes sparsely planted along the edge of the burn and they used these as part of their hides.

The decoys went out next but that was a major problem. The shell shapes were there but there were no pegs to hold them in position and it was quite windy. They cut sticks out of the bushes taking three or four cuttings from each bush not causing too much damage. It took a long time and by the time all the decoys were pegged up it was breaking light. As the light broke the rain started and the wind picked up in strength. We sat in our hide and it gave some shelter from the rain. The trouble was the decoys kept blowing over and two of them blew into the burn. Dad kept running out and pushing the pegs into the ground but it was a continuous job.

Light had completely broken now and there was still no sign of the geese. There was another heavy shower though and the wind picked up again dislodging four of the decoys. It was while dad and Tony were out seeing to them that I heard the sound of geese in the distance. I looked at dad and Tony and they obviously hadn't heard them because they were busily pushing the sticks into the ground. I could still hear the geese and then I saw them in the distance. They were heading in our direction and dad and Tony were still out there tidying up the decoys. I didn't know what to do and decided to let out a little bark. Dad shouted at me to be quiet and just carried on with his job. I could see the geese clearly now but they were not making a lot of noise like the pinkfeet were the previous morning. They were about a quarter of a mile away when thank goodness The Greg heard them. He shouted to dad and Tony and they both came scurrying back bent right over. Dad put some cartridges in his gun and pushed in tight against the hide.

The geese were coming from behind us and were flying into the wind and rain. If it hadn't been for the rain I am sure they would have seen dad and Tony out on the grass field. If they couldn't see them well they certainly wouldn't have seen the decoys, so I was thinking that it was a bit of a waste of time putting them out there.

The geese were in just one skein flying in the perfect formation but they were quite high. As they came over us they must have seen the decoys because they seemed to become more excited and were making far more noise. They were probably about sixty yards high and nobody fired a shot. After they had flown over the decoys they swung round in a big arc loosing height all the time. They swung out into the field behind us on the other side of the burn and came over us again, but much lower than before. The Greg was in the centre and he fired first with both barrels but never touched a goose. The skein split and started to climb as dad and Tony fired at them. They hit one goose each almost at the same time. The goose that dad hit crashed down in the field out in front of us but Tony's goose seemed to climb into the wind and then fell backwards, landing in the burn. It was dead but it was floating away with the flow.

'Get on!' was the order from dad. I ran along the bank of the burn until I was in front of the goose and then I leapt into the water. It was freezing but I don't think I noticed that until afterwards. I was soon next to the goose and the damn thing was nearly as big as me. I got hold of one of its wings and started to swim towards the bank. It was hard work and by the time I had reached the bank the current had taken me another fifty yards downstream. I dragged the goose up the muddy bank and when I reached the level field I tried to get a better grip of it. I got hold of the bottom of its neck and carried it back. Dad was delighted with me and after making a fuss of me he sent me for the one in the field. This one was not as big as the other goose and I had no problem taking it to him.

We waited another hour but nothing else came. They collected the decoys in and we headed back for the Jeep. Grob was not very pleased when he saw the geese and hardly spoke to me on the way back to the hotel.

When we arrived back there was a telephone message from mum. The Greg's partner had informed her that The Greg's boss had broken his leg while skiing and had been flown home early. He would like to know where his Jeep is.

That was the premature end to my first goose shooting trip in Scotland and an hour later they were packing the Jeep for the drive back to England. Tommy said to dad, 'See you again old pal. And by the way, I was joking about the ferret's teeth, you ken.' We were then on our way home for another eight hours of Grob's snoring.

CHAPTER 9

Keeper's day with Laurel and Hardy

It was nearing the end of the season and dad had been invited to a keeper's day. This is the day when the beaters and the picking-up brigade, who have contributed their efforts throughout the season, are invited to take their guns, and the people who usually shoot wisely stay well away.

Dad knew that he would be invited and I heard him telling mum that he was definitely going to refuse. He told her that some of the beaters didn't have a clue how to shoot properly and were dangerous, because they insisted on shooting at low birds. There was no way he was going this year to any keeper's days because last year he was nearly shot.

When the keeper rang him offering the invitation he immediately said without hesitation. 'Thank you very much I would love to come. It is very kind of you, and I will be there before nine-thirty.' When he put the phone down mum said to him. 'I thought you were going to refuse the invitation.' He replied, 'Well, you know how it is. I didn't like to let him down because he relies on me and a few others to make up the bag.' I thought to myself, the rest of them must be rubbish shots if they are relying on him.

On the day of the shoot it was a crisp frosty morning. Dad had to scrape the ice off the car windscreen before we set off. He put his gun on the back seat with the packed lunch. He must have been expecting a good day's shooting because he had six boxes of cartridges on the seat as well.

The sun was very low and he had to keep stopping to clean the windscreen every ten minutes. He had forgotten to put some antifreeze in the washers and they were frozen solid. Every time he stopped he was cursing and I was getting fed up of listening to him. I was looking forward to the day though, because I knew I would have a mixture of picking up for the standing guns and hunting with the walking guns. I also had something else well implanted in my mind. The place where we were going to was where I had met that gorgeous black Labrador dog called Jet. It was almost love at first sight but I had not seen him since and I often think about him. I was very much hoping that he would be there today.

We eventually turned off the road and onto the track which leads to the farmyard. This track is littered with extremely deep potholes and the last time we were on it dad was cursing because every time the car wheel dropped into a hole the car was bottoming on the track. This time all the holes were full of water, which had frozen over, and it was like a skating rink. There is quite a deep drainage ditch situated along the side of the track and as we came to the first bend we ended up in it. The car slid off the track and down the sloping side of the ditch, rolling onto its roof in the bottom. Dad was hanging upside down in his seat belt and the cartridges were scattered all over the place. He managed to release his seat belt and fell onto his head, which I quite enjoyed. He said, 'I knew I shouldn't have come today. I had a feeling things would go wrong.' As far as I could see the only thing that went wrong was that he was driving too fast and couldn't see properly through the dirty windscreen. Still, he won't have to clean it again because it is now in a million pieces.

He managed to push the door open and climbed out, spending the next five minutes trying to remove the particles of glass from his hair and clothing. I managed to shake mine out in one go. He was trying to collect the cartridges when Tony's vehicle stopped on the road above us. Tony got out and looked down saying, 'Nice bit of parking Vince! Are you and Bess okay?' Up to that point I don't think it had entered dad's head to check if I was all right. He looked at me and then replied, 'Talk about the luck of the Raw. I think we are okay but the car might be a write off.' Tony said, 'Wouldn't it have been better to park it in the farmyard like you did last time you were here?' Dad looked up at Tony and said, 'Okay smart arse! Are you going to help me or just stand there taking the piss?' I could see Grob looking out of the window with a big grin on his face. Tony was trying not to laugh but couldn't help a smile as he said, 'There is a small layby just around the bend. I shall park in there before someone runs into me.'

He parked up and then walked back. He helped dad collect all the cartridges up and they put them in a bag. Tony said, 'You're a bit of an optimist aren't you? Last year when I was here on keeper's day I fired just ten shots.' Dad just ignored him and tried to salvage what he could from the remains of the packed lunch. He put his gun slip over his shoulder and they walked away from the car.

After a little while he stopped and turned to look at the car again. It looked in a sorry state lying on its roof with its wheels in the air.

Dad then said, 'If it was pulled out very carefully I think it might be repairable.' He had no sooner said it when a Landrover came along the track and started to slide on the same patch of ice as dad's car had. The Landrover slid to the edge of the track above dad's car and stopped just in time with its wheels right on the edge. Dad said, 'Bloody hell, that was close! Who is it in the Landrover anyway? I wonder if he could tow my car out?' Tony replied, 'His name is John. He picks-up with rather a large spaniel. John is a bit of a snob but you could ask him.'

As Tony spoke, a red van came into the bend going far too fast. I heard dad shout, 'Oh no!' as the van collided into the side of the Landrover with enough momentum to push it over the edge, and it slid down crunching into dad's car. John, who was still inside, pushed the Landrover door open and struggled out. He just stood there staring at the carnage. I knew I had seen him before but I couldn't remember where. He then worked his way to the back of the Landrover and opened the door. A large black and white spaniel dog jumped out which I recognised straight away. It was Podgy my big brother.

The man driving the van was Wally with the potbelly. The van had quite a dent on the front wing but at least it was still on the track. John started to complain to Wally but he just replied, 'Don't be so bloody stupid John. It isn't anybody's fault, it is the ice on the track.' He then took a bag out of the back of the van and said, 'I am going up the track a bit to warn the others or we all end up down there.' He then walked back the way he had come waving the bag as he went. Tony said to John, 'Get your gear together and put it in my Jeep. We will have to get the tractor to pull the vehicles back on to the road later.'

I walked over to Podgy and said, 'Do you remember me?' He looked at me and said quite rudely, 'Why should I?' I replied, 'Because you spent the first six weeks of your life trying to bite my ears off, and the last time I saw you, you had just peed down your dad's trousers.' He turned and stared at me for a few seconds and then said, 'You are my sister. I remember the dodgy bloody markings on your face.' Hardly a compliment but I thought I would ignore the remark and said, 'Yes I am your sister and my name is Bess. My dad comes beating here and brings me with him. Tell me all about yourself. It is great to see you again.' He sort of frowned and looked down on me as he said,' My name is Simon and I do not work with beaters. I only pick-up and usually at far better places than this. My dad only picks-up here once a season so he can get an invite to keeper's day. We work mostly on the better estates. And by the way, don't tell the others that you are my sister.' I couldn't believe what I was hearing. I said to him, 'I love you too Podgy.' He replied angrily, 'If you ever call me that name again I will bite your ear off and make a proper job of it.' He then walked away from me with his nose in the air. What an arrogant dog he has turned out to be. I have heard people say that a dog's nature is often like that of their dads. I hope that is not the case with me. I would hate to complain all the time like my dad does. I wouldn't mind being like my mum though. She has lots of patience.

While we were getting into Tony's Jeep there were several more vehicles driving past, but all extremely slowly. Wally had done a good job. When we arrived at the farmyard there were quite a lot of people there. Some I knew and some I didn't. I saw Paddy, the Irish water spaniel, and ran over to him. He said,' Hello there Bess. Don't forget to keep your fecking head down for the end of the season blast. I don't think Jack is coming so there shouldn't be too much fecking fighting today.' I said, 'Have you seen Jet?' He replied, 'I haven't seen him for quite a while.'

I walked back to stand with dad but I was straining my eyes looking for Jet. There seemed to be dogs all over the place and twice I saw a black Labrador and my heart slumped as both times I realised that it wasn't Jet.

Another van pulled into the yard and a man got out. My heart started thumping again as I knew that this was Jet's dad. He walked over to a group of men and they were discussing the road conditions and what a mess the vehicles were in that had slipped off the road. I was waiting for him to open the back door of the van so I could see Jet but he just carried on talking. He eventually opened the side door and started to put on his leggings and coat. Maybe Jet isn't with him, I thought. Maybe he had run away because of the regular beatings he got with the stick.

Just when I had given up hope he opened the back door. He picked up a stick out of the van and then said, 'Come on you!' A dog jumped out of the van and to my sheer delight it was Jet. He was a couple of years older but just as handsome. He looked around the yard and caught my eye. I smiled at him and he sort of half smiled and then turned away. Maybe he hadn't recognised me, I thought, so I ran over to him. He saw me coming but he looked very serious. I kissed him and said, 'I have missed you Jet. How are you?' He replied, 'I am okay Bess, but I think it would be better if you forget about me.' I was shocked and said, 'I don't want to do that Jet. What is wrong?' He just stared down at the ground and said, 'I can't tell you Bess, but believe me, it would be better if you just go now.' After he said that his dad hit him with his stick and said, 'Come on you! We are going to start,' and then they walked away. I was really upset and Jet never even looked back.

I couldn't understand what was wrong with him. When I saw him before he was so happy and friendly but now he was sad and miserable. Maybe he has met someone else, I thought. If he has she doesn't seem to have made him very happy, that is for sure.

Hardy came out of the house and started to get things organised. The men drew strips of card and were divided into two teams. I was hoping Jet would be in our team but he wasn't. Podgy was though and he was rapidly becoming a nuisance. He had bitten two dogs already and we hadn't even started. Grob was in our team as well as Paddy.

On the first drive our team were to be the walking guns. This is basically a beater with a gun in his hand, and in some cases it is an extremely dangerous mixture. Any birds that get up and fly forward towards the standing guns should be left to fly over them. Any birds flying back can be shot at by the walking guns. Seems simple, but unfortunately so are most of the beaters, and it doesn't always work like that.

Today there were two tractors with trailers, for want of a better word, and the two teams had one each. The other team went off in their trailer. As it pulled out of the yard I could see Jet sitting in it. He didn't look at me though. He was just staring at the floor.

At the end of the drive I saw him again. He was carrying a pheasant back to his dad but with very little enthusiasm. I stood watching him and I just couldn't believe the way he had changed.

When the picking-up was over I went to him again. He saw me coming and said, 'Bess, I told you it would be better if you stay away from me.' I replied, 'I know you did Jet, but you never told me why. I think a lot about you and I need to know what is wrong. Maybe I can help.' He looked at me and I could see his eyes filling up with tears as he said, 'I don't want to tell you why because I don't want to upset you.' A tear rolled down his cheek and dripped onto the ground.' I said, 'It's a bit too late to worry about that Jet. I am already upset. I think you should tell me whatever it is.'

We were both crying now as he said, 'Okay Bess. I will tell you at lunch time. There won't be enough time now as they are about to start again.' I kissed him and said, 'Try not to worry Jet. Things are often not as bad as they seem, but please tell me something before you go. Have you fallen for another dog?' He kissed me gently and said, 'No Bess, it's not that. I have never wanted another since I met you.' Dad shouted my name and I left Jet looking more miserable than ever. What on earth can have gone wrong to make him so sad?

It was our turn to stand and the tractor dropped us off at a field gate. We walked up a hill and then lined out in a valley behind a wood full of fir trees. John was on our right and Podgy was sitting next to him. Tony and Grob were on our left and Grob kept looking across.

The pheasants started coming over and the shooting started. After a while dad shot a cock bird that dropped behind. He said, 'Get on!' I ran back to retrieve it and was about to pick it up when Podgy charged into me knocking me over. I lay there for a few seconds as he had winded me. He said to me, 'I do the picking-up around here so just leave them for me.' He then picked up the pheasant and ran off. I limped back to dad and he looked at me as much as to say, where is it?

Dad shot another two on that drive and each time Podgy was there to chase me away. When the drive was finished Grob came over and said, 'That spaniel over there is a bit rough isn't he? I think I will have a word with him.' I said, 'Don't worry about it Grob. I know him.' He said, 'I saw him stealing your birds Bess.' I replied, 'I know he did but it doesn't bother me. It isn't worth arguing about.' I didn't want Grob to say anything because Podgy was an aggressive dog and I didn't want Grob to get hurt.

Lunch time at last and we were in the barn. Most of the dogs were busily scrounging some food but I had lost my appetite. Jet walked over to a corner and I followed and lay next to him. I said to him, 'I know it is difficult for you but please tell me now.' He started trembling and his bottom lip was shaking as he said, 'My future is very uncertain Bess. Very, very uncertain.' 'Why is it?' I asked. 'Tell me why?' He sat up and took a deep breath as though he was trying to keep control and said, 'On the Sunday, which is a week tomorrow, my mum and dad are emigrating to Australia.' My heart seemed to sink to the bottom of my stomach but I tried to put on a brave face and said, 'You must not worry too much. I have heard it is nice there, and you might like it.' He took another deep breath and said, 'You don't understand Bess. They are not taking me with them.' I looked shocked and asked, 'Why not?' His eyes started filling again and he looked down at the ground as though he couldn't look at me as he said, ''This has been planned for quite some time. I heard them talking and they said that the quarantine period and the airfare for me was far too expensive.' 'So what is happening to you Jet?' I asked. He was really choking up now and struggling to speak as he slowly said, 'At first they were going to try and find someone to look after me, but I heard them talking the other day and they haven't managed to do that. They are now considering the other two alternatives.' As he said that he stopped talking and choked up again. I said, 'I know it is difficult for you but please tell me what they are.' The tears were flowing down his cheek now and his bottom lip was trembling out of control as he said, 'They are trying to make up their minds whether to put me in a dog's home or to have me put to sleep at the vet's. You can now see what I mean about my future Bess. I am only six years old and there is nothing wrong with me. I think it will be the vet's though because I heard them saying that it would be the cheapest way.' I was shocked and said, 'They can't do that to you.' He sighed and replied, 'I am afraid they can Bess, and they probably will.' 'What is the matter with them?' I asked, 'Don't they love you?' He replied, 'No they don't love me Bess. They have never shown any affection. I work hard for him but I usually get belted a few times with his damn stick when we are out. When we are at home I live in a shed. I suppose I shouldn't complain because it is dry and I get a bowl of food every day.' I said, 'I just can't understand it. Both my mum and dad love me.' He forced a smile and said, 'You are very naive Bess. I know hundreds of dogs that are jealous of you. Not many dogs live in your lifestyle.' I said, 'There must be something we can do Jet. Can't we run away together?' He replied, 'That wouldn't work Bess, and why would you want to run away from the perfect home?' I interrupted him and said, 'Because I want to be with you Jet.' He went on to say, 'No Bess, it just wouldn't work. There is nothing that we can do about the situation and that is why I didn't want to tell you. I want you to go home and forget about me.' I kissed him and said, 'I will never forget you and I know that isn't what you want.' We just lay there together for a few moments and then we had to go out for the afternoon shooting session. For the first time in my life I had no interest in the hunting or picking-up so I won't even tell you about it.

When we arrived back in the farmyard after the shooting had finished the action started again. Grob had seen the way Podgy had been treating me and decided he was going to do something about it. He went over to Podgy and said something and they started fighting. Podgy was getting the better of Grob so I ran over and shouted, 'Leave him alone Podgy.' He climbed off Grob and swung around to face me and said, 'I told you what I would do if ever you called me by that name.' He ran across and sunk his teeth into my ear. I squealed and then Jet moved in. He flipped Podgy over and started to bite him. Podgy was outclassed as Jet bit him several times. Podgy was now lying in a submissive position on his back and Jet was standing over him. He was about to go in with another bite when I shouted, 'Don't hurt him any more Jet. Please don't hurt him. Jet said, 'I have been watching him Bess and he has been horrible to you all day. I am going to teach him a lesson he will never forget.' I pleaded again, 'Please don't hurt him Jet.' He looked at me and said, 'What's wrong Bess? Do you fancy him?' I said, 'No Jet! He is my brother.'

When Tony dropped us off mum looked worried. Dad told her about the car in the drainage ditch and never stopped blaming everything and everyone except himself. I went straight into my basket in the kitchen and just lay there. I couldn't stop thinking about poor Jet. I think mum was fed up with listening to dad because after a while she said, 'The car was on its last legs anyway Vince. I have managed to save some money so why don't you go out tomorrow and buy that little Jeep you have always wanted? I saw a nice one today in the garage at the bottom of the hill.' He replied 'What a good idea! I think I will.'

Mum put my food down but I couldn't eat it. I had a strange feeling in my stomach but it wasn't hunger. I spent the next four days just lying in my basket and never ate a thing. I went into the garden to do my toilets but I didn't even want to go for a walk.

Dad bought his Jeep and he was happy. It just didn't seem at all fair to me. Dad made a total mess of things through his own stupidity but now he is happy. Poor Jet has done nothing wrong and tried to be the perfect dog, and through no fault of his own he is going to be put to sleep in two days' time on Saturday. His mum and dad fly out on Sunday and I hope their conscience bothers them. Although I don't think it will.

On Thursday afternoon mum was stroking me. She said, 'What is the matter with you Bess? You haven't eaten anything since Saturday.' I just wished I could have told her. I am sure she would have helped. She then said to dad, 'Take Bess to the vet's Vince. I am sure there is something wrong with her.'

Dad took me to the vet's and on the way there he said, 'What do you think to the Jeep Bess?' I usually wag my tail when he speaks to me but I just ignored him.

The vet examined me thoroughly and then said, 'I can't find anything wrong with her.' I knew that even a good vet couldn't diagnose a broken heart. He stuck a needle in me anyway and charged dad twenty pounds and we went home again.

I think dad was starting to feel sorry for me because on Friday he went out shopping and came back with a new basket for me, putting it next to the one I was lying in. He does stupid things like that sometimes but I couldn't see the point in it because there was nothing wrong with the one I had. I couldn't sleep at all on Friday night. I spent the whole night crying, knowing that it would be the last night that Jet would be alive. I thought of him lying in his shed just like being in a condemned cell.

After dad had eaten his breakfast on Saturday he put his coat on. He looked at me in my basket and said, 'I am going out Bess. Do you want to come?' I just lay there and ignored him. Mum bent down and started stroking me again. She said, 'There is definitely something wrong with Bess!' Dad replied, 'She probably knows what is happening. Dogs can often sense things that are going to happen. Anyway I had better be off.' He went down the stairs and I heard his Jeep drive away. Mum said to me, 'How I wish I knew what was troubling you Bess.' I thought, how I wish I could tell her.

Early Saturday afternoon I heard dad's Jeep pull onto the drive. Mum was in the kitchen and looked out of the window. She said, 'Your dad is back Bess.' I just stayed in my basket and I had decided I would starve myself to death. Mum went out of the kitchen and closed the door behind her. I heard her say hello to dad as he came up the stairs.

He opened the kitchen door and I sat up in my basket in pure shock. He had a dog lead in his hand and on the other end of the lead was Jet. I must have looked stupid as I could do nothing but stare. Dad said, 'I hope you don't mind Bess, but this fellow is going to come and live with us.' I ran over to Jet and kissed him and he had tears of joy running down his face. I was so elated I started tearing around the kitchen floor and after about six laps mum grabbed me and told me to settle down. I suddenly realised who the other basket was for. I don't think Jet had eaten anything for a week either because we both ate a massive dinner that night.

Living with Jet is absolutely wonderful. He is so kind and gentle and we love each other dearly. Dad takes us to the shoots together and we work as a team. I don't have to worry about aggressive or randy dogs any more because Jet is always with me and the other dogs all respect him. Jet doesn't get hit with a stick any more and he is enjoying life to the full.

I don't think mum and dad have bargained for cross Labrador and spaniel puppies but I am becoming extremely broody, and I am sure that it is only a matter of time. I know Jet will be the perfect father.

Vince Raw welcomes your comments
e-mail: gallowaycottages@aol.com